EAT YOURSELF SMART

EAT YOURSELF SMART

CHARLIE AYERS

WITH KAREN ALEXANDER AND CAROLYN HUMPHRIES

DK

London New York Munich Melbourne Delhi

Project Manager and Editor: Norma MacMillan
Project Art Editors and Designers: Smith & Gilmour, London
Photographer: Noel Murphy

Managing Editor: Dawn Henderson
Managing Art Editor: Heather McCarry
Editor: Ariane Durkin
Production Editor: Jenny Woodcock
Production Controller: Sarah Sherlock

First published in Great Britain in 2008 by Dorling Kindersley Limited
80 Strand, London WC2R 0RL

Penguin Group (UK)

Copyright © 2008 Dorling Kindersley Limited
Text copyright © 2008 Charlie Ayers

Google is a trademark of Google Inc.

2 4 6 8 10 9 7 5 3 1

A CIP catalogue record for this book is available from the British Library.

ISBN: 978 1 4053 2804 3

Printed and bound in China by Sheck Wah Tong Printing Press Ltd.

Discover more at
www.dk.com

CONTENTS

WELCOME TO MY WORLD

SMART CHOICES

You're smart. So why don't you eat that way? /// 10
Fast, Raw, and Organic /// 12
Go organic /// 14
Eat it raw! /// 26
A fascination with fermentation /// 38

THE SMART LARDER

Your larder. A cook's database /// 42
You are what you freeze /// 64
Our refrigerators, ourselves /// 74
More kitchen essentials /// 96

SMART RECIPES

Start my day /// 106
Take a break /// 136
Winding down /// 186
Pick me up /// 230

Index, suppliers, and acknowledgments /// 250

WELCuME Tu MY WuRLu

// I WAS HIRED TO FEED GOOGLE INC. BACK IN NOVEMBER 1999, WHEN THE COMPANY WAS YOUNG AND SMALL, AND HUNGRY FOR PROGRESS. CO-FOUNDERS LARRY PAGE AND SERGEY BRIN WERE LOOKING TO PROVIDE THEIR EMPLOYEES WITH FAST, UNFETTERED ACCESS TO CLEAN, HEALTHY, DELICIOUS FOODS. THEIR GOAL WAS TO NOURISH THE BODIES AND BRAINS AND SPIRITS THAT WOULD PROPEL THEIR FAST-GROWING COMPANY FORWARD. THEY WANTED POWER FOODS THAT WOULD LEAVE THEIR MINIONS STIMULATED AND ENERGETIC AFTER LUNCH, NOT SLUMPED OVER THEIR KEYBOARDS. AND THEY WANTED IT DONE WITH THE HIGHEST QUALITY ORGANIC, SUSTAINABLE-SOURCED INGREDIENTS IN AN ENVIRONMENT THAT MADE THEIR BRAINY, ECLECTIC EMPLOYEES FEEL LIKE A FAMILY.

// I was employee number 53 at Google, and even though I really wanted the job I thought Larry and Sergey were crazy when they hired me. Sergey told me that Google would grow to be tens of thousands of employees. I laughed. "Some of the best restaurants in Palo Alto are all around you," I said. "Go there." Sergey said that was not very efficient – it takes away from their productivity to have everyone going out to eat. Those Google guys (in the beginning, they really were all guys) were curious and adventurous, and wanted exciting flavours. They were from all parts of the country, and all over the world. They were young, most of them recently out of school, and they worked all the time. They missed their families and they missed their mamas' cooking. They were eating burritos and pizza every day because they barely had time to shower, much less worry about what to eat.

// When I left Google in May 2005, I had five sous chefs and 150 employees working for me in 10 cafés across the company's sprawling Mountain View, California, headquarters. We were serving 4,000 lunches and dinners daily to a team of people as diverse and hard-working as any on the planet. I learned so much from my family of clients at Google. Inspired by their sense of adventure, and blessed with the incredible bounty of clean, sustainable, amazing foods available here in California, I came to believe that we can all eat delicious, clean, fast cuisine that is good for us, good for the community, and good for the Earth. I want to help people eat better, and if we don't have a lot of time, then let's do it quickly.

I WANT TO HELP PEOPLE EAT BETTER.

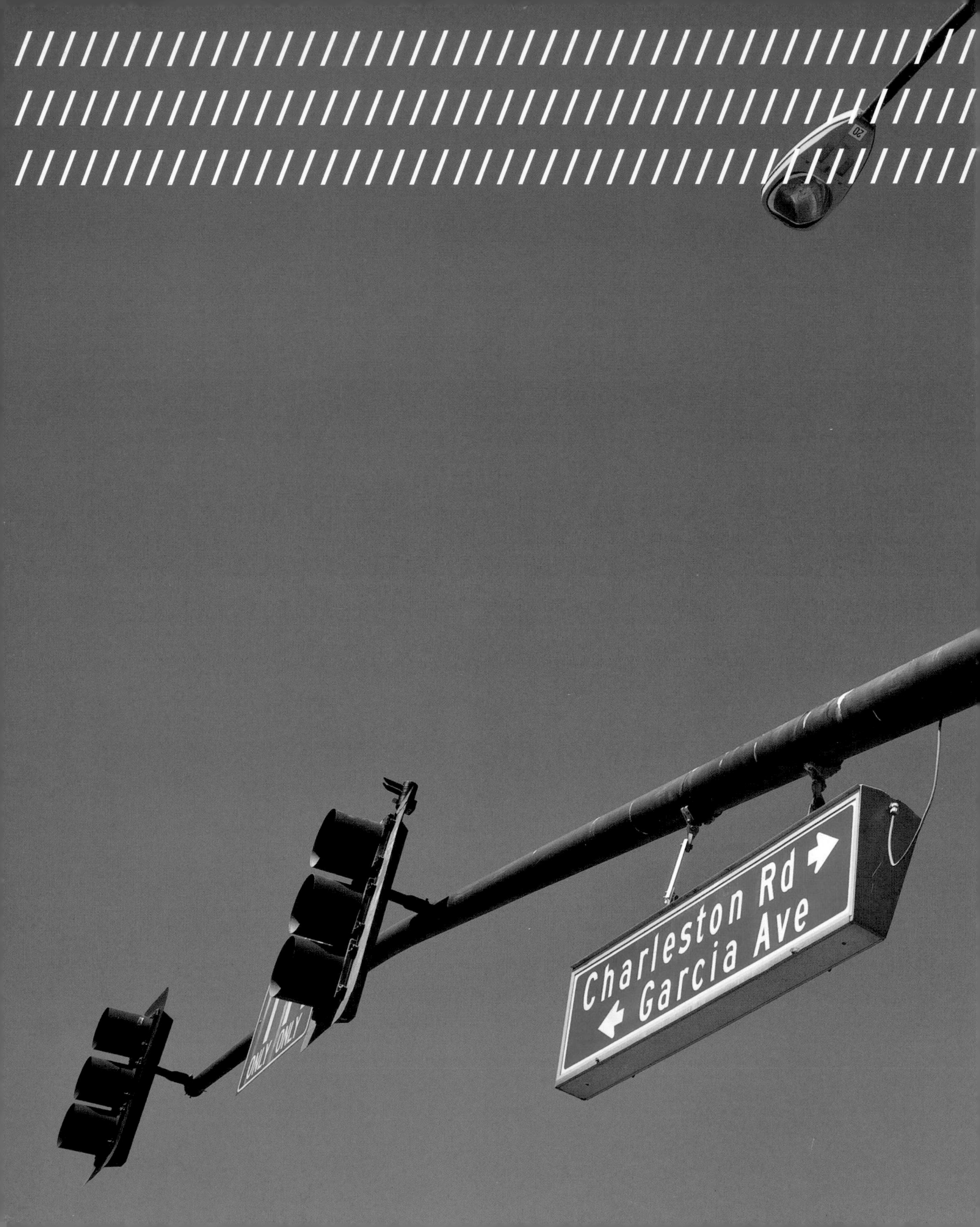
Charleston Rd
Garcia Ave

///
///
////////////////////////////////: SMART CHOICES

YoU'RE SMAĸT. SO WHY DON'T YOU EAT THAT WAY?

// I BELIEVE THIS GENERATION HAS SUCH AN OPPORTUNITY TO EAT WELL AND DO IT THE RIGHT WAY, BUT MOST OF THE TIME WE'RE JUST BLOWING IT. PEOPLE ALWAYS THINK, WELL, I HAVE TO EAT SOMETHING QUICKLY SO IT HAS TO BE BAD FOR ME. MY ANSWER TO THAT IS, WHY?

// Each snack and each meal you eat is an opportunity to make a difference – in your body and your world. At Google, Sergey and Larry believed that if everyone was eating healthy and eating well, they were going to have healthy, productive, happy, and efficient engineers working for them. It made sense for them as a business investment, even if there were cheaper alternatives available, and it makes sense for you, too. Invest in yourself. Make smart choices, eat great food, and reap the dividends.

EACH MEAL IS AN OPPORTUNITY TO MAKE A DIFFERENCE – IN YOUR BODY AND YOUR WORLD.

FAST, RAW, AND ORGANIC.

THAT'S WHAT I'M THINKING WHEN I COOK

// **Fast.** Food does not need to be unhealthy to be prepared quickly. Some of the healthiest, most delicious foods are straight out of nature and don't take any time to prepare.

// **Raw.** You don't have to eat raw at every meal. After all, this is a cook book! But raw food is great for you, and despite my years of experience as a chef, I continue to find that often the best thing you can do to a good piece of food is to leave it alone.

// **Organic.** Be intelligent about your food. Organic, clean, sustainable farmed food is imperative. But not all organic food is equal. If something is imported from far away, or comes swathed in too much packaging, it's not clean at all. It has probably done more harm than good to the environment – your environment – en route to your mouth.

GO ORGANIC

// JUST BECAUSE THERE'S AN "ORGANIC" STICKER ON MY APPLE DOESN'T MEAN IT'S ALWAYS THE BEST CHOICE. I BELIEVE WHOLEHEARTEDLY IN CHOOSING ORGANIC PRODUCTS WHEN THEY'RE AVAILABLE LOCALLY, BUT GIVEN THE CHOICE BETWEEN AN ORGANICALLY GROWN APPLE THAT CAME OFF A CARGO JET FROM CHILE AND A PIECE OF IN-SEASON FRUIT THAT WAS GROWN LOCALLY WITHOUT PESTICIDES, I'LL CHOOSE THE LOCAL FOOD ANY DAY.

// Getting smart about your food involves taking a little extra time to consider the impact of what you're eating – on yourself and on your environment. It means investing a few extra minutes with the shopping trolley or the restaurant menu to learn more about what you're buying. Once you get into the rhythm of shopping that way and you become familiar with the best local food sources available in your area, it really doesn't take much time at all.

// There's a lot of highly processed junk food in the supermarket made with organic ingredients. And a lot of otherwise clean, wholesome products come wrapped in an obscene amount of nonrenewable packaging that will be jamming the landfills for decades to come. Just because a cream cake is organic doesn't mean you should eat it.

THERE'S A LOT OF HIGHLY PROCESSED JUNK FOOD MADE WITH ORGANIC INGREDIENTS.

3 QUICK RULES FOR HOW TO EAT

1 READ LABELS

2 ASK QUESTIONS
3 CONSIDER YOUR OWN VALUES

ORGANICS: WHY THE "BIG O" MATTERS

// Organics are not the only path to clean, smart food. But the Big O still reigns supreme. Organic, locally sourced food is the ideal. Why? Because most of the chemicals used on nonorganic foods are byproducts of petroleum, which is not a good ingredient for recipes. That's nasty, and I don't know why it's considered okay to feed people like that.

// Even food that is totally pesticide-free may have been grown with synthetic fertilizers that are unhealthy for the soil, the local environment, and you. Organic means the soil is clean, the water is clean, and your food is clean. It means you get less poison for your money.

// What's your inner voice saying to you? Does it matter, or doesn't it matter? You can take all the information that's presented to you and make a reasonable decision about whether the actions you're taking are going to have that big of an impact. Sometimes you might indulge in something a little naughty, but if you eat clean most of the time you won't feel so guilty when you slip up a little bit.

ORGANIC SIMPLY MEANS TRYING TO AVOID CRAP IN YOUR FOOD.

READ THE LABEL

// Check the label. If it doesn't sound like food, it probably isn't. The ingredients listed first are the ones that are most plentiful in a product. For example, in breads and cereals, you should always look for whole grains at the top of the list. Wheat flour is not a whole grain unless it says "Wholewheat Flour."

LOOKING FOR THE PUREST FORM OF AN INGREDIENT IS THE BEST APPROACH

///

> For juices, this means making sure it says "not from concentrate".
> When shopping for beef, or dairy products from cows' milk, look for "grass fed".
> When purchasing eggs from chickens, ducks, quail, and geese, look for "pastured eggs".
> If you are buying oils, look for "cold-pressed" and "unrefined".
> Shopping for beer, wine, and alcohol, look for small batch distilleries, locally microbrewed beer, and boutique wineries.

///

IF IT DOESN'T SOUND LIKE FOOD, IT PROBABLY ISN'T.

STUFF TO AVOID
FEEDING TO YOURSELF OR PEOPLE YOU LOVE:

PESTICIDES
HYDROGENATED OILS
CORN SYRUP
REFINED SUGARS
THE PRESERVATIVES SODIUM NITRATE AND SODIUM NITRITE
THINGS YOU CAN'T PRONOUNCE

BE NOSY

// The easiest way to make sure you're eating smart is to ask questions of the people who are selling you food – in the supermarket or the market or the restaurant. Be nosy. Make friends with your local shopkeepers and stall holders. Build relationships with them so you're comfortable asking them questions and they're comfortable telling you the truth.

// I'm nosy. At restaurants, I stick my head in the kitchen to see what's going on. I've gone behind restaurants and looked in the garbage to see what they were using. This one guy said he wasn't using ketchup in his Korean barbecue sauce. I wanted to know what was in it, so I pulled up behind the place and I saw a big can of ketchup in his dustbin.

GOOD QUESTIONS TO ASK THE PEOPLE WHO SELL YOU FOOD
///
> Where was this grown or raised?
> Was it treated with pesticides?
> When did this shipment arrive?
> What's in season right now?
> Are you expecting any great deliveries that I shouldn't miss this week?
> Can you recommend something delicious to go with the fresh wild salmon I just bought?
///

AT RESTAURANTS, I STICK MY HEAD IN THE KITCHEN TO SEE WHAT'S GOING ON.

KEEP IT LOCAL

// I like to impose a 240-kilometre (150-mile) travel limit on my food as much as possible. If you buy food that has been grown or raised locally, it will be fresher, cheaper, and more delicious. It will have generated a lot less pollution and earth-warming greenhouse gases on the way to your mouth. What's more, buying local products will help sustain and nourish your local marketplace to ensure that bountiful fresh, local, clean food will continue to be available to you.

// Where I live, in the San Francisco Bay Area, you don't need to go further than a 240-kilometre (150-mile) radius to get anything – except coffee beans, bananas, and the ingredients to make chocolate. We live in the midst of a wonderful cornucopia of bounty, from fish and meats and dairy to produce and wine. I can even buy local lemongrass and ginger now. Still, there are always going to be some things that by nature call for an exception to the rule, such as the exotic curry powders and spices and sauces I buy from various ethnic markets. Although you won't always be able to find what you're looking for locally, it pays to ask. Going to your local farmers' market is a tremendous way to learn about what your region has to offer.

FOOD GROWN OR RAISED LOCALLY WILL BE FRESHER, CHEAPER, AND MORE DELICIOUS.

APPRECIATE THE SOURCE

// One of my primary goals at Google was teaching people to appreciate how their food was produced. Because all of my delicious food was served free to Google employees, I wanted to make sure they were not taking it for granted. I wanted them to understand what kind of thought and resources had gone into growing it; I wanted to establish a connection between the land and the people who ate from it – even if they worked in cubicles and played roller hockey on a concrete parking lot. If I could make smart eaters out of people, I could help make them into smart citizens and smart consumers, too.

// Often, we'd be lucky enough to discover a personal connection to a terrific crop of something special. Googlers loved food that had a story behind it, and when they knew it was from someone in their own society they were even more excited about it. That always reminded me how important it is to take the time to learn the stories behind our food. When we appreciate its source, we are enhancing our own ability to enjoy it and make the most of what we eat.

// One Googler's dad grew figs out in Modesto. One day I got to work and opened my big refrigerator to find six boxes of gorgeous figs sitting there. I was baffled, until I got this email from him later in the day: "I brought you some figs." I called them "the prized Kamangar figs" after this guy, Salar Kamangar, and his dad who had grown them, and we celebrated them for a week at a time when they were in season.

TAKE THE TIME TO LEARN THE STORIES BEHIND YOUR FOOD.

EAT IT RAW!

// SOMETIMES, THE BEST WAY TO COOK FOOD IS NOT TO COOK IT AT ALL. RAW FOODS ARE ESSENTIAL TO PRESERVING AND FORTIFYING THE DIGESTIVE ENZYMES FOUND IN OUR BODIES, WHICH CAN BECOME DEPLETED AS WE AGE. NATURAL ENZYMES THAT OCCUR IN RAW FRUITS AND VEGETABLES ARE DESTROYED BY COOKING AND PROCESSING FOODS, WHICH IN TURN REQUIRES OUR BODIES TO USE UP MORE OF OUR VALUABLE ENZYMES DIGESTING THOSE FOODS. DIGESTIVE ENZYMES ARE ESSENTIAL FOR THE BODY TO PROPERLY UTILIZE NUTRIENTS AND VITAMINS, SO WHEN THEY ARE DEPLETED WE CAN EXPERIENCE A LACK OF ENERGY, OR EVEN DIGESTIVE PROBLEMS.

// At Google, where maintaining the diners' energy was a key goal of my cooking, I made sure I offered at least two raw salads every day. The ingredients received no heat whatsoever.

// Eating raw foods just makes me feel alive. I actually get a buzz from eating sushi. And there's no better way to save time making a meal than to skip the cooking part altogether. Just be sure to always wash fruits and vegetables extra thoroughly before eating them raw, even the packaged ones like those "prewashed" bags of salad.

YOU CAN SAVE TIME AND ENZYMES BY EATING RAW FOODS.

FRUIT. PLAN AHEAD

// Except for the occasional banana, no one would eat fresh fruit at Google unless I had peeled it and cut it up for them. Are we all really that lazy? Maybe we're just too busy to bother.

// Sadly, I'm not going to be there to cut your fruit for you every day, so you've got to think ahead and do it for yourself – before you're hungry.

HOW TO MAKE SURE YOU EAT FRUIT
//
> Keep a tub of cut pineapple, mango, papaya, berries, or melon in the fridge all the time.
> Apple slices will keep nicely in a bag in the fridge if you first toss them in water with a little bit of lemon juice added, then drain them and pat them dry.
> Strawberries and stone fruits (peaches, plums, apricots, and nectarines) get mushy if you cut them in advance. Wash them up thoroughly as soon as you get them home, and you'll be able to grab a mouthful of sweetness whenever you're feeling hungry.
> Whip up a quick smoothie or toss a couple of handfuls of fresh fruit into your yogurt in the morning.
> Layer pear or apple slices onto your sandwiches.
> Toss a handful of berries on your salad.
> Make a fruit salad salsa (see opposite) to spoon on top of fish or poultry. I like to serve this salsa over my lobster tacos.
//

RECIPE // FRUIT SALAD SALSA

> Combine 150g (5oz) seedless watermelon diced small (about ⅓ of a melon, depending on its size), 2 jalapeño peppers diced with seeds (or 1 serrano pepper), a handful mint leaves cut into ribbons, a handful very roughly chopped coriander leaves, 150g (5oz) diced red onion, lime juice to taste, and cracked black pepper. Add salt at the very last moment, because the salt draws out the liquid from the melon and makes a watery mess.

IT PAYS TO HAVE YOUR OWN JUICER. SHOP-BOUGHT FRUIT JUICES ARE PASTEURIZED, AND THEY LOSE A LOT OF FLAVOUR AND NUTRIENTS IN THE PROCESS.

VEGGIES. YOU CAN'T LIVE WITHOUT THEM

// Keep crudités in your fridge at all times, ready to go – while you're listening to music, or waiting for your dinner to cook, just cut up a huge bag of vegetables. Make carrot and celery sticks, and jicama and cucumber spears. Wash up some cherry tomatoes. On a lazy day, all that and a bowl of hummus or guacamole can pass for a meal!

// One exception: Don't eat raw cauliflower or raw broccoli, because your body doesn't digest them well and you won't get the whole nutritional value out of them. But don't overcook them either. If you blanch them lightly, they'll keep that delicious crunch and the flavours will peak, too.

RECIPE // A GREAT SALAD TO KEEP IN THE FRIDGE

> Toss together some jicama, radishes, lime juice, and a little cayenne pepper. Then drop in some orange segments. In a salad I try to go for that sweet-salty-sour synergy and I want to be sure it's going to have some crunch to it. This one hits all those elements at once.

DRINK YOUR GREENS

// Wheatgrass is great for cleansing the blood of toxins. It also contains strong digestive properties, making it a good choice for those with slow digestion or constipation. If taken before a meal, wheatgrass helps you digest your meal properly and move it along through your system. If taken after a meal, your body is more likely to absorb its nutritional values.

// Now I'm a wheatgrass believer. The stuff just makes you feel alive. Good, fresh wheatgrass has a sweet finish to it, and you feel great after you drink it. I think the people at Google got into it because they saw that we were willing to be goofy with them to get them to try new things. I didn't mind putting on a show to get people to do something good for them. I recommend drinking wheatgrass straight up, not adding it to anything else.

// Some people do experience some unpleasant effects from drinking wheatgrass (such as diarrhoea and headaches). If this happens more than a couple of times after you first start incorporating wheatgrass into your lifestyle, then you are either taking too much or it's simply not for you.

// I had never been a fan of wheatgrass before, but one of the cooks who worked for me at Google was this big surfer from Santa Cruz, and he loved it. He convinced me to offer wheatgrass shots in the vegetarian section of the café, and it took off like crazy. I had one woman who did nothing but trim wheatgrass, grind it up, and pour it into shot glasses. We even had a little bell you could ring after you downed a shot. Drinking this thing that was good for you just became part of the culture, and pretty soon we were grinding up 250 shots a day – 20 boxes of wheatgrass – and the bell was going off all the time.

RAW JUICE SNACKS

// Raw juice drinks will keep you feeling alive and pure – all the hippies in Northern California love them!

// If you purchase fruits and vegetables already prepared, the prep time for these drinks will be far less than if you start with whole produce, but if you enjoy saving money, buy them in their entirety. To make things easy, use a high-quality vegetable juicer, something that can stand up to lots of abuse.

RECIPE // BEET-CARROT-GINGER FIZZ

> Juice 3 peeled carrots, 1 peeled large, fresh beetroot, and 1cm (½ in) peeled piece of fresh root ginger. Pour over ice in a glass. Top off with sparkling water, stir, and sip through a straw.

RECIPE // CARROT-CUCUMBER LEMONADE

> Juice ⅓ peeled cucumber and 3 peeled carrots. Mix with 2 tsp fresh lemon juice and chill. Drink this cold (no ice), garnished with a thin slice of cucumber.

RECIPE // CARROT-CELERY-APPLE JUICE

> Juice 2 peeled large carrots, 2 celery sticks and 1 cored apple. Chill. Garnish with a small stick of celery, if you want, and drink cold (no ice).

RECIPE // CARROT-GINGER-ORANGE JUICE

> Juice 4 peeled carrots, 2.5cm (1in) peeled piece of fresh root ginger, and 2 peeled large oranges. Chill. Drink cold (no ice). This is good with vodka – it's the sassy cousin to Screwy Rabbit (see page 114).

RECIPE // CARROT-PARSLEY JUICE

> Juice a handful of fresh parsley, including the stems (I like the curly leaf for juicing and flat-leaf for cooking), and 4 peeled large carrots. Chill. Drink cold (no ice), garnished with a sprig of parsley.

RECIPE // SPICY TOMATO-CELERY-LIME

> Juice 1 peeled small lime, 1 small, fresh jalapeño chilli (seeded or not, depending on how much fire you want), 2 large, ripe tomatoes, and 2 celery sticks. Pour over ice in a chunky glass and garnish with a slice of lime. You can add vodka for an evening reviver!

RECIPE // THREE-MELON CRUSH

> Juice ¼ each cantaloupe, honeydew, and Crenshaw melon (all peeled and roughly cut up). Pour over crushed ice in a large glass. Experiment with other combinations of melons, too.

RECIPE // PINEAPPLE-GRAPEFRUIT JUICE

> Thinly pare a strip of zest from 1 ruby red grapefruit and cut in thin strips. Peel the rest of the fruit. Juice the grapefruit and 1 small pineapple (peeled and sliced). Pour over crushed ice in a large glass and garnish with the grapefruit zest.

RAW FISH. BUY IT, CUT IT, EAT IT

// Fish is brain food, fact. I remember in the early days, before I started serving dinner at Google, Sergey would order up platters and platters of sushi from some local high-end sushi joint. He often came downstairs to the café, where I was busy cleaning and preparing for the next day's lunch, to share some with me. I thought it was pretty nice of him to remember me down there.

// Maybe Sergey just loved sushi. Or maybe he loved sushi because he knew that fish is super high in Omega-3, which is a crucial fatty acid we need in our daily diets. The fat found in fish helps make the cell membranes found in the brain more elastic and more able to absorb nutrients easily, which aids in brain development early on in life and then helps maintain the ability to learn new things as we grow older. These fats help to create stems to other cells. As I see it, fish is a great source for this natural lube we need to keep our minds up and running, ready to receive and respond.

// Raw fish is especially easy to prepare. I think it is best served sashimi-style, in small, thin slices with a soy-based dipping sauce, or as a carpaccio (see my recipe for tuna carpaccio on page 155).

// If you are buying and serving it yourself, the best raw fish to prepare at home is tuna. Pretty much all of the tuna available on the mass market has been frozen previously – unless you're buying it at the harbour. Cold-smoked fish is also a healthy, delicious choice. I generally advise leaving raw oysters and other kinds of raw fish to restaurant professionals.

HOW TO BUY THE FRESHEST TUNA TO EAT RAW

//

> If it's a whole fish, make sure the eyes are clear, not cloudy.
> Poke at the flesh. Does it spring back, or does your finger leave
an indentation? You want fish that springs back quickly.
> Look for tuna that is a bright, deep red. Avoid fish that is greying
or that has an oxidized rainbow look.
> Be sure to ask when and where it was caught, and when your
fishmonger received it.

//

FISH IS A GREAT SOURCE OF THE NATURAL LUBE WE NEED TO KEEP OUR MINDS UP AND RUNNING.

A FASCINATION WITH FERMENTATION

// ACROSS THE GLOBE, EATERS HAVE FIGURED OUT THAT FERMENTATION IS A GREAT WAY TO EAT. FROM PICKLED GINGER WITH SUSHI AND INDIAN PICKLED MANGO WITH CURRY TO DILL PICKLES WITH A PASTRAMI SANDWICH, FERMENTED FOODS ARE DELICIOUS. AND THEY CAN SERVE A VITAL PURPOSE IN PROTECTING YOUR HEALTH.

// There are plenty more fermented foods we eat on a daily basis that we all love and don't even realize they are fermented. Bread, yogurt, cheese, and even chocolate all undergo fermentation. And drinks? Tea, coffee, wine, and my choice – beer – are fermented, as is miso paste, a particular favourite of mine. At Google I made enormous vats of Korean kimchi (see the recipe below, given to me by my friend Nina Kim). Everybody loved it.

// A custodian of your gastrointestinal track, fermentation works to keep your insides clean by helping to fight off microorganisms in your food and giving you a healthy constitution, so to speak.

RECIPE // NINA'S KIMCHI

> Toss a large head of Chinese cabbage, cut in bite-size pieces, with 2 tbsp kosher salt, then drain in a colander for 3 hours. Rinse well, drain, and dry. Mix with 4 sliced spring onions, a handful of chopped coriander, 1 tbsp each black and white sesame seeds, 60ml (2 fl oz) rice vinegar, the juice of a lime, 1 tbsp toasted sesame oil, and 2 tbsp (or more) *sambal oelek* in a nonreactive bowl. Cover and let marinate at least overnight (it gets better over a week's time). This makes about 675g (1 ½lb).

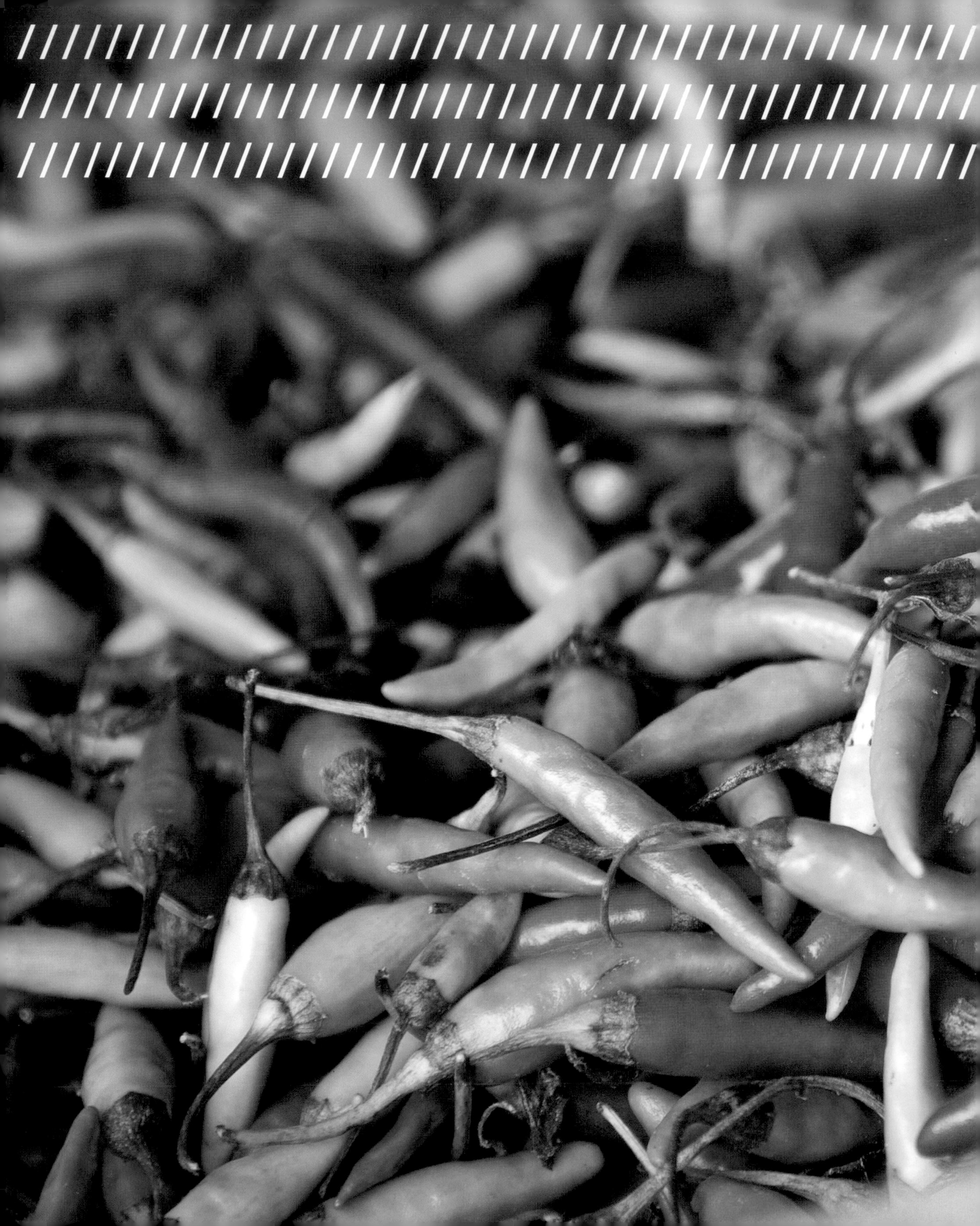

THE SMART LARDER

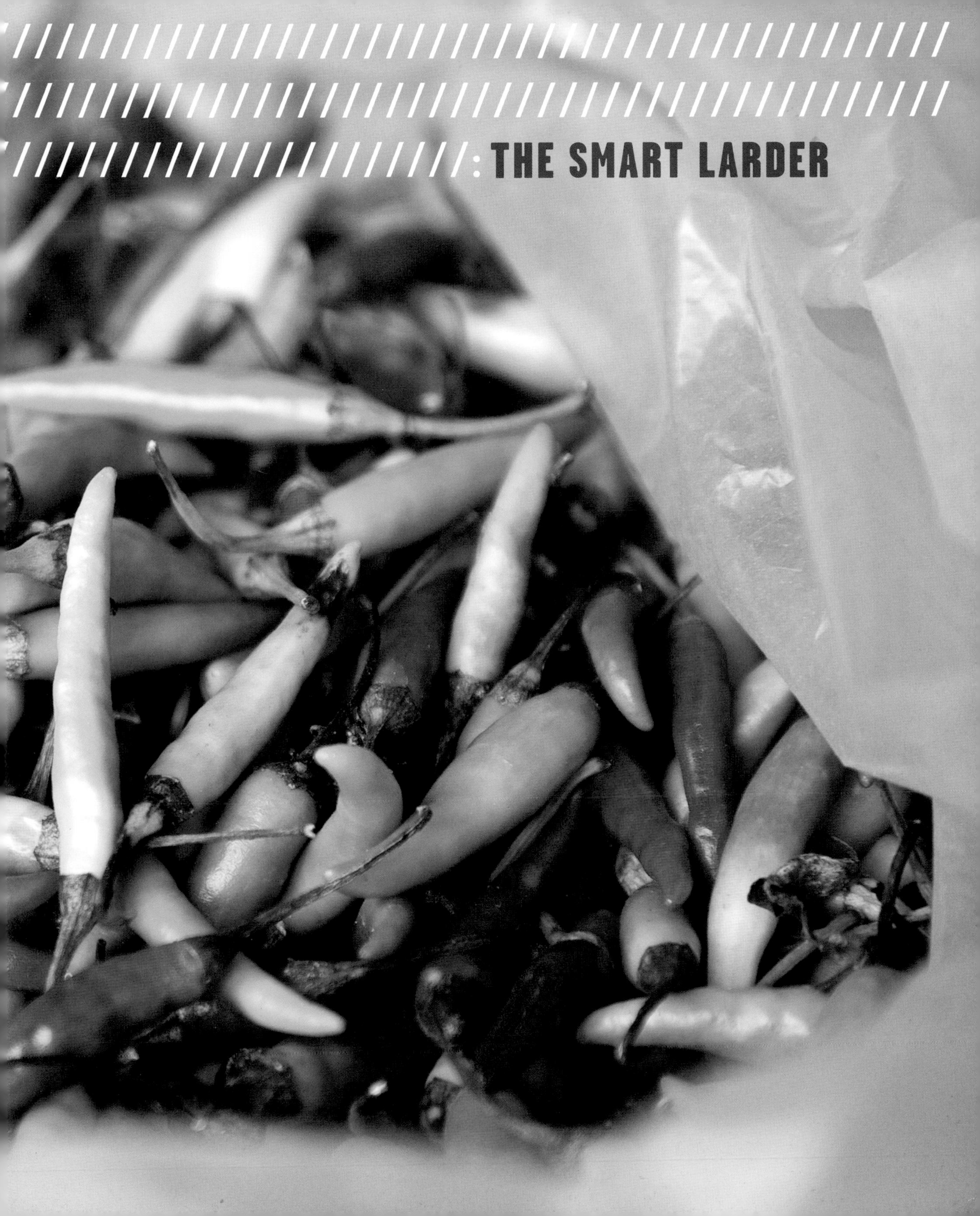

YOUR LARDER.
A COOK'S DATABASE

// I'M A CONSTANTLY CURIOUS COOK, SO I'M ALWAYS WILLING TO TRY OUT NEW THINGS AND EXPERIMENT ON MYSELF FIRST. IF IT GOES WELL, I'LL TRY IT OUT ON OTHERS. I SHOP AT A LOT OF ETHNIC MARKETS BECAUSE THEY OFTEN HAVE REALLY GOOD DEALS AND I CAN FIND THINGS YOU WOULDN'T SEE ANYWHERE ELSE. WHEN I GET THE CHANCE TO VISIT A NEW SHOP, I HEAD FOR THE CONDIMENTS SECTION FIRST TO CHECK OUT WHAT KINDS OF VINEGARS AND OILS AND SALTS AND SPICES THEY HAVE. I'M ALWAYS EAGER TO FIND SOMETHING I'VE NEVER SEEN BEFORE.

// My wife, Kimmie, is really good about being willing to taste new things. I try to cook for my family as much as possible, and so they get to try out a lot of the weird stuff I find. My larder is where most of my eclectic purchases end up. It's my cooking database, so to speak. I'll try something out, and even if it's not right I'll remember the flavours and try it again later on something else. I think a diverse and well-stocked larder is the key to being a quick, versatile cook.

I FIND A LOT OF GREAT WEIRD STUFF IN ETHNIC MARKETS.

VINEGAR. THE UNSUNG HERO OF FLAVOUR

// Good, tasty vinegar can be the crowning glory to your dish, a zesty shot of flavour that helps brighten all the other surrounding tastes. I have 20 or more vinegars in my larder. It's one of my favourite things to buy, and I find that having several different vinegars on hand offers me a lot of flavour flexibility when I'm working on a new dish.

// When cooking meat or chicken, the sweeter, fruity vinegars are great for deglazing your pan to create a nice *au jus* sauce. I'll just add a little bit to the hot pan juices and stir it up. No additional heat is necessary, and it will blend right in to create a delicious sauce. It reduces rapidly and has a great intense flavour. But don't add too much or your whole dish will taste like salad dressing.

VINEGAR NEEDS GREAT FLAVOUR THAT WON'T OVERPOWER THE FOOD.

MY 4 FAVOURITE VINEGAR PAIRINGS

1 APPLE CIDER VINEGAR
OR BALSAMIC-FIG VINEGAR WITH PORK

2 CHINESE BLACK VINEGAR WITH
STIR-FRIED BEEF

3 RICE VINEGAR WITH STEAMED
SEA BASS OR TUNA

4 UME PLUM VINEGAR WITH
ROASTED TURKEY LEG

TOP FAVOURITE VINEGARS I USE MOST FREQUENTLY AT HOME

//

> **Chinese black vinegar.** I use this in the base of many different Asian or East Asian-influenced dishes.

> **Japanese ume plum vinegar.** It's wonderful in a cold composed salad made with fresh sweetcorn and barley.

> **Rice vinegar.** Makes a wonderful dipping sauce for tempura vegetables.

> **Red wine vinegar.** Perfect for your basic French vinaigrette with shallots and Dijon mustard.

> **White wine vinegar.** Chardonnay, Champagne, and Muscat are all good for deglazing and making quick pan sauces.

> **Banyuls vinegar.** This is a good finishing vinegar for that sweet and sour profile.

> **Apple cider vinegar.** Use it in pork brine or turkey brine recipes.

> **50-year-old aged balsamic vinegar.** Use it for finishing over grilled meats. Balsamic-fig vinegar is worth looking for.

> **Sherry vinegar.** Good for Spanish-influenced dishes, roasted mushrooms, game birds, and polenta.

> **Brown rice vinegar.** I use it in place of rice vinegar when I'm looking to add that crunchy hippie twist to a recipe.

> **Malt vinegar.** Duh. It goes on fish and chips.

//

RECIPE // VANILLA-INFUSED VINEGAR

> Score a vanilla bean several times, then lightly toast it in a nonstick pan, just until it becomes fragrant. Drop it into a bottle of high-quality, mild vinegar (apple cider vinegar works well; or you could use rice vinegar). Close tightly and let steep for 2 weeks. Then begin to explore its flavours.

VINAIGRETTES

// I love to make my own vinaigrettes. Your basic ratio for vinaigrette is one part vinegar to three parts oil. Sometimes I'll add a little bit of fruit juice that matches and pairs well with the particular flavour. It can help take the edge off your vinegar and keep it from tasting too intense.

// Depending on how fancy you want to get, you can always add some spices or ginger, garlic, or shallots to give your dressing extra depth. I like to toast cumin or coriander seeds and grind them fresh into a vinaigrette. Or, you can make a reduction using some shallots and ginger or garlic and a little fruit juice. When it's reduced by half, remove it from the heat and hit it with the vinegar, right in the pan. Let it cool, and whisk in the oil.

RECIPE // ORANGE-MISO VINAIGRETTE
> Mix 1 tbsp white miso paste, 250ml (8 fl oz) fresh squeezed orange juice, 1 tbsp minced pickled ginger, 1 tsp mustard powder, 3 tbsp canola oil, and 1 tsp toasted sesame oil in a bar blender. Serve over roasted beetroot and rocket with crispy shallots, garnished with black and white sesame seeds. Seared ahi tuna served rare goes well with this.

RECIPE // LEMON-SHALLOT VINAIGRETTE
> Combine the juice from a lemon, 1 tsp Dijon mustard, ½ tsp red wine vinegar, and 1 tsp minced shallots in a bowl. Whisk in 4 tbsp extra virgin olive oil and add salt and pepper to taste. You can add any fresh herb – chives, thyme, tarragon, chervil – or add them all and make it a Green Goddess dressing.

RECIPE // WASABI VINAIGRETTE
> Throw 3 tbsp rice vinegar, 2 tbsp wasabi powder, 4 tbsp mayonnaise, ½ tsp each toasted sesame oil, lime juice, and tamari, 1 tsp black sesame seeds, and 1 ½ tbsp minced spring onion in a glass jar. Close the top and shake away. Serve this over slightly grilled endive and frisée, alongside pan-roasted salmon or shrimp.

SALTS

// Salts from different regions around the world often have very distinct flavours, textures, and smells, which can really work to enliven and authenticate the flavour of different ethnic cuisines. I love tasting the different minerals in salt and trying to imagine where they came from. The shades of pink and grey can be very beautiful.

// Remember to season your food inside and out for a consistent flavour all the way through. If you're cooking a chicken breast, you need to season the stuffing and the inside and outside of the chicken equally. Season the flour for coating, too. With salt and seasonings, you are creating layers of flavours. You are assigning your food a texture and a smell, and you usually want that to be consistent throughout the dish.

// But how much salt? I think too much is when you can taste salt before you can taste what it is that has been salted. Of course, if you are supposed to be watching your sodium intake for health reasons, don't cheat. Protect your health first, your flavours second, so you can keep cooking and eating good food for a long time to come.

WHEN TO LAY OFF THE SALT
///
> I avoid salting mushrooms while cooking them as this helps to give them a really nice colour. If you salt your mushrooms in the pan, all the juices exude from them and you end up with a pan of mushroom liquid and poached mushrooms rather than pan-roasted or sautéed.
> I don't put salt in a marinade.
> Never add salt to the water you are cooking your beans in.
> Salt tends to make root vegetables too mushy, because the pores in the vegetable tighten when cooking in salted water. If you cook your root vegetables in unsalted water, you're allowing them to take in the water and cook evenly from the inside out, rather than the other way round.
///

OILS. NOT JUST FOR COOKING

// Oils can go rancid pretty quickly in the larder. If you don't use them often, you might consider storing them in the fridge if there's space. If you do refrigerate your oil, you will need to leave a little extra time for it to return to room temperature before you pour it.

THESE ARE MY FAVOURITE OILS

///

> **Olive oil**. I use high-quality extra virgin olive oil only for finishing a dish, or in a vinaigrette. For cooking purposes, save your money and use regular olive oil, or canola or grapeseed oil.

> **Citrus oils**. I keep several different kinds of concentrated citrus oils, which I use to add a bright shot of flavour without having to drag out the citrus juicer. They are great for raw marinades, and for layering in flavour at the end of cooking. A very small amount goes a long way. Try adding a splash of orange oil to your vinaigrette to serve with Belgian endive or watercress salads, or add a drop or two of lemon oil to marinades for lamb or fish.

> **Rice-bran oil**. I've recently been turned on to this oil, which is great because it has absolutely no flavour. It's good for infused oils or vinaigrettes, when you want to taste everything else, but not the oil.

> **Toasted sesame oil**. I only use sesame oil in very small amounts. It smells good, but I find it can easily overpower the food.

///

CHEESE-FLAVOURED OILS

// I make my own deliciously flavoured oils by infusing them with cheese rinds. Olive oils infused with Spanish Manchego cheese or Parmesan are two of my favourites. Make the oils in small quantities. If you're not going to use them up quickly, they should be refrigerated. After six months or so, you need to start all over with a fresh sterile bottle and add new cheese rinds and flavourings to fresh oil.

RECIPE // MANCHEGO OR PARMESAN OIL

> Stuff cheese rinds saved from Manchego or Parmesan cheese into a sterilized wine bottle and add a couple of cracked black peppercorns, coriander seeds, fennel pollen (which you can order online), and bay leaves. Or add strips of orange or lemon rind instead – it depends on the flavour you're looking for. Pour in olive oil. Cork the bottle back up and let it sit for several days before using.

GREAT WAYS TO USE CHEESE-FLAVOURED OIL

///

> Dress organic baby rocket and roasted beetroot – unbeatable with Parmesan cheese oil – and season with a small amount of kosher salt and freshly ground black pepper.
> Toss in at the end of a pasta dish.
> Drizzle over steamed fish.
> Use as a dipping oil for fresh bread.

///

THE GRAIN GAME

MY FAVOURITE GRAINS
//
> **Millet**. This is bird food to everyone else, but I love it. Boil it up and add it to soups or stews, or to vegetarian chilli, about an hour before the dish has finished cooking. It blossoms nicely to fill out the dish, making it more substantial and satisfying.
> **Corn meal**. White for grits (see page 255), yellow for polenta.
> **Farro**. Also known as emmer, this ancient strain of wheat is far more durable than its cousin durum, which is more commonly consumed around the world. Farro is widely eaten in Umbria and Tuscany in Italy – the über pastamaker will tell you that wheat flour derived from farro is the best to use when it comes to pastamaking. Look for it in specialist shops and online.
> **Quinoa**. Great in soups, stuffing, and salads, and it makes a nice pilaf. Even better, quinoa is the only grain that is also complete protein. Always rinse quinoa thoroughly before you cook it or else it will have an offensive odour after it cooks.
> **Kamut**. I like kamut cold in a salad with dried fruits, fruit juices, cinnamon, and ginger. It's one of my favourite combinations.
> **Barley**. Even though pearl barley doesn't have a whole hell of a lot of nutritional value, it adds real body and substance to a lot of dishes. Used sparingly, I think barley is silky and satisfying.
//

RECIPE // CHEESE GRITS
> Put 230ml (8 fl oz) each milk and water (or all water for a less creamy finish) in a heavy-based pan with 1 tsp kosher salt and some black pepper and bring to a boil. Gradually whisk in 175g (6oz) stoneground white grits. Turn the heat to low, cover, and cook, stirring occasionally, until thick, about 15 minutes. Stir in 130g (4½oz) shredded sharp Cheddar cheese and 1–2 tbsp butter, plus some Google hot sauce (see page 249) or other hot sauce, if liked. Serves 4

NUTS AND SEEDS

KEEP THESE FOR MIXING INTO COOKING OR SALADS, AND FOR GENERAL MUNCHING

//

> Almonds
> Pistachios
> Toasted hemp seeds
> Sunflower seeds
> Pine nuts
> Cashews
> Black and white sesame seeds

//

FLAX SEED

> We all know flax seed is super healthy for you, but it has to be toasted and worked carefully into a dish or it will taste gritty – and you walk around with what looks like sand in your teeth all day. I use flax seed mostly in muffins and pancakes.

IT'S TRUE THAT NUTS AND SEEDS ARE HIGH IN FAT, BUT IT'S MOSTLY THE HEALTHY TYPE.

EAT YOUR BEANS

// I've always appreciated the flavour and texture of beans. There's something calming and relaxing and settling about a good dish of beans. While there are producers of good organic canned beans, I tend to favour the texture of dried beans in my cooking when there's time.

// You have to remember to soak dried beans overnight or they won't be ready to go when it's time to cook. Even letting them soak all day while you're at work is usually good enough. But if you forget, you can cheat. All you have to do is boil the beans quickly in a pot of water, then cover them, remove from the heat, and let them soak for about an hour. Drain away the liquid and you're ready to go.

// When it comes to cooking the beans, it's a good idea to boil rapidly for the first 10 minutes to remove any toxins before reducing the heat to simmer them until they are tender.

NEVER ADD SALT TO YOUR BEANS WHEN THEY'RE COOKING. IT HARDENS THEM UP AND THEY NEVER FULLY COOK.

BLACKEYED PEAS.
BLACK BEANS.
KIDNEY BEANS.
SPLIT PEAS.

I EAT CARBS

// Have you noticed that everyone who was on the Atkins diet is now off it? Carbs – pasta, bread, and rice – are back. In particular, pasta is a quick, fast-cooking food that yields high returns. I just try not to abuse it and eat it too much. My advice is, be smart. If you're eating pasta, don't also eat bread with your meal.

// I keep a lot of different kinds of rice around. Brown rice is nutty, slightly chewy, and aromatic – just amazing all on its own when fresh from the rice cooker. I'm also a big fan of the parboiled basmati rice that I buy from an Indian supermarket near me. Parboiled rice takes less time to prepare, and it cooks up more evenly.

MY TIPS FOR COOKING AND EATING PASTA
//
> I use really salty water to boil my pasta. You don't want just a sprinkle of salt. You want it to be noticeable in your water so the pasta absorbs that salty flavour.
> You can make a really good, really fast pasta tossed with canned tuna, canned tomatoes, capers, and lemon.
> I buy sealed packages of fresh lo mein noodles from the refrigerator section at the Asian supermarket. They're addictive. I cook them up spicy with garlic and chilli paste, and end up eating the whole pan of noodles.
> You're free to experiment with wholewheat pasta. No doubt it's better for you, but I've tried it and I just can't find one I like.
//

COOKING RICE

> People often cook rice too quickly. If it is really boiling rapidly, the water evaporates too soon and your grains end up mushy. You want to go for a long, slow boil. A good rice cooker makes that easy. You might have to play around with it a little to get the right amount of liquid for each kind of rice, but once you figure this out a rice cooker really does the job nicely.

TURN UP THE HEAT

// If you like spicy food, as I do, you'll appreciate a wide variety of hot sauces in your larder. I have friends from cooking school who make some crazy hot sauces that you have to sign a waiver just to buy. I'm not that nuts, but I do like having the option of turning up the heat when I cook.

// At Google, hot food – like a lot of other things – became a kind of geeky macho thing. It was their rite of passage, so they just sucked up my hot sauce. It's so hot you wouldn't want to eat it straight. I use it as a base for other things. It was a tremendous recipe that started with 6 pounds of habaneros, 2 pounds of jalapeños, and 14 dried chipotles. Do not worry. I've scaled it down for you (see the recipe on page 249).

// I'll use ready-made hot sauces in my recipes, primarily to save time – and so I'm not burning up my eyes mincing chillies all the time. I really like Sriracha Hot Chilli Sauce, a Vietnamese-style product that comes in a squeezy bottle with a rooster on it. You can find it at most Asian markets or order it online. At Google, we used so much of this chilli sauce that we referred to it as "special red sauce #2." Special red sauce #1 was ketchup.

// This Google guy Dan O'Brien gave me a batch of chillies in 2002, which his dad had grown in New Mexico. One little flake was like fire. I had this whole big bag full of them, and now they're almost gone.

CHILLI-HOT VINEGAR

// You can use chilli peppers to make your own spicy vinegars, which you can use like Tabasco sauce. I was on a spicy chicken wing kick for a while, and for them I made some great, fiery vinegar using about three dozen packets of chilli flakes that I had left over from the pizza delivery guy! This made a huge batch of vinegar, but you can do it with a much smaller amount of chilli flakes (the amount you use depends on the level of pain you can endure, and the type of chilli flakes).

// Here's the trick: I put some of my batch into a squirt bottle. As the chicken wings came out of the oven, I deglazed them right in the pan with my chilli vinegar. The vinegar melded beautifully with the pan juices to make a perfect spicy chicken wing sauce.

// But a stern safety warning: Keep your head far away from your oven-hot pan when you are dousing it with your homemade pepper spray. When that vinegar hits the heat, it steams up into a sizzling cloud of tear gas. You don't want your eyes or nose anywhere near that situation. I learned that the hard way.

RECIPE // CHILLI-INFUSED VINEGAR

> Toast about 1 tbsp chilli flakes in a pan, then grind them up in a coffee grinder. (A very important note: Only do this if you keep a separate grinder for spices. Otherwise, your coffee will forever taste like pepper spray.) Funnel the powder into 230ml (8 fl oz) vinegar, add 1 tsp salt, and let it sit.

RECIPE // HOT CHICKEN WINGS

> Heat a frying pan, then toss in the desired amount of wings plus some salt and pepper and a small amount of ketchup or hot chilli sauce. Give the wings a good coating, to get some colour on them, then roast at 200°C (400°F) for 20–25 minutes. Return them to the stove top. Turn up the heat. Shake your chilli-infused vinegar and give the wings a good squirt. Stir with a wooden spoon, then remove the wings with tongs to a serving dish. Finish the sauce with a small amount of beer and 2–3 tbsp butter, and serve it with the wings. Drink the remaining beer with the wings.

PEOPLE GET HOOKED ON CHILLIES BECAUSE THE BRAIN RESPONDS TO THE BURNING TASTE BY RELEASING ENDORPHINS THAT MAKE YOU FEEL HAPPY!

TO GET THE MOST FROM SPICES: BUY THEM WHOLE IN SMALL QUANTITIES, STORE THEM IN A COOL PLACE OUT OF THE LIGHT, KEEP THEM IN AIRTIGHT CONTAINERS AND GRIND THEM YOURSELF

SPICES

// Don't buy one of those huge discount containers with a lifetime supply of ground cinnamon. Spices lose their punch quickly – within six months. And when you're buying a spice blend, such as curry powder, try out a few to find out what you like. Their flavours can vary dramatically.

HOW TO TOAST AND GRIND YOUR OWN SPICES

///

> Preheat a nonstick frying pan over medium heat.
> Toast your spices for 1–2 minutes, tossing them in the pan just until it starts to lightly smoke and you can smell the fumes rising off the surface.
> Remove from the heat and transfer the spices out of the pan immediately or they will continue to burn.
> Grind them in a coffee grinder, or for small quantities, grind with a mortar and pestle.
> If you don't have a grinder or mortar and pestle, sandwich the toasted spices between a piece of folded greaseproof paper, and return it to the cooled pan you used for toasting. Smash the spices up with your hand, and rub them around in a circle a little bit to release their essence.

///

RECIPE // SOUTHWESTERN SPICE RUB

> Mix together 3 tbsp ground annatto seed or paprika, 60g (2oz) each unrefined granulated sugar and salt, 2 tbsp ground cumin, 1 tbsp ground caraway, 2 tsp each turmeric and onion powder, 1 tsp each habanero chilli powder and ground black pepper, and ¼ tsp celery seed. Store in an airtight container in a cool, dark place. Use for any grilled or pan-fried meat, chicken, or fish.

YOU ARE WHAT YOU FREEZE

// YOUR FREEZER IS THE BEST WAY TO MAKE SURE YOU ARE EATING HEALTHY AND CLEAN, EVEN WHEN YOUR NORMALLY BUSY LIFE SHIFTS INTO OVERDRIVE. KEEP THE FREEZER FULL AND WELL ORGANIZED — JUST LIKE YOUR LIST OF EMAIL CONTACTS — SO YOU WILL ALWAYS HAVE WHAT YOU NEED AT YOUR FINGERTIPS WHEN YOU WANT TO EAT SOMETHING GOOD, AND FAST.

THE COLD FACTS

///

> A full freezer is important. If it's not full, it's not running at maximum efficiency. You can save energy – and unnecessary car trips to the shops – by keeping your freezer insulated with lots of good things to eat.
> Make your own convenience food. You will save money, and eat better.
> Label and date your frozen foods, and keep an eye on what's in there to make sure things don't get too old. The best way to do that is skip the cooking at least once a week and eat something from the freezer.
> If you're serious about your freezer, invest in a vacuum-pack sealer so you can freeze your food airtight and fresh, without bulking up your freezer with a bunch of clunky plastic containers. Remember that removing the air from bags and containers is vital to prevent oxidation of the food, which will cause it to turn brown.

///

MAX FREEZER STORAGE TIMES

///

> Fruit and veggies: 12 months
> Meat and poultry: 12 months
> Fish: 3 months
> Smoked fish: 2 months
> Bread: 6 months
> Cooked rice: 6 months
> Cooked beans and pulses: 12 months
> Cooked pasta (undercooked or it will be too soft on thawing): 2 months
> Stock: 3 months
> Sauces: 3 months

///

FREEZING VEGGIES AND FRUIT

///

> Buy what's in season, and store it for darker days.
> Sealed bags of precut vegetables are a great thing to have in the freezer –
but only if you plan on cooking them. Don't freeze veggies you expect
to eat raw. And unless you blanch them first, only store for a week or two.
> Small bags of frozen chopped onions are a great time-saver.
> Green beans, broccoli, cauliflower, asparagus, peas, and sliced
mushrooms all freeze well.
> Making a stir-fry? Chop double the vegetables and freeze half for next time.
> Frozen berries are fabulous in a smoothie and don't need to be thawed first.

///

FREEZING COOKED GRAINS AND BEANS

//

> Nothing speeds up a stir-fry like having the rice already cooked and ready to go. Keep small sealed bags of cooked brown rice in the freezer for a healthy accompaniment to your stir-frys.
> For a satisfying, no-effort side dish, reheat 350g (12oz) frozen cooked rice with an ice cube of chicken stock, a drizzle of olive oil or a knob of butter, and some herb salt (see page 93).
> Frozen cooked beans are good to add to a quick pot of chilli or soup.
> A handful of cooked lentils or pearl barley can up the heartiness of practically any stew or soup. Add them in the final stages of cooking so they don't become overcooked.

//

LABEL EVERYTHING CLEARLY. THERE'S NOTHING WORSE THAN THAWING OUT A PACKAGE OF WHAT YOU THOUGHT WAS PASTA SAUCE TO FIND THAT IT'S BREAD SAUCE.

FLAVOUR CUBES

// These are a quick way to add depth and flavour to your recipes. Fill ice cube trays with juice – carrot, beetroot, or lemon, for example – or soup stock or another preparation. When they're frozen, transfer the cubes to an airtight bag. Then toss a cube or two straight into a dish as you cook. Here are some of my favourite cubes for flavouring soups, sauces, or casseroles. Freeze them for up to three months.

// Some whole food shops and websites sell awesome little trays of frozen chopped herbs and crushed garlic produced by Kibbutz Dorot in Israel. The tiny little cubes pop right out of the tray, and in cooked recipes you would never know the herbs and garlic had been frozen.

RECIPE // GARLICKY CHILLI-CHICKEN CUBES

> Combine 1l (1¾ pints) good chicken stock, 2 tbsp puréed garlic, 1 tbsp dried chilli flakes, 2 tbsp long grain rice, and 60g (2oz) peas (blanched fresh or thawed frozen). Bring to a boil, then simmer to cook the rice. Purée in a food processor or blender (it's okay if it's slightly lumpy). Let cool, then add some chopped fresh mint or basil. Pulse one more time to purée the herbs (it will be a sexy green colour).

RECIPE // MOROCCAN CARROT-HARISSA CUBES

> Boil 2l (3½ pints) carrot juice to reduce by half. Toast 2 tsp caraway seeds with 1 tsp cumin seeds until fragrant. Add 1 tbsp dried chilli flakes and toast for another minute, then add 175g (6oz) roasted aubergine purée, 1 tbsp each puréed garlic and fresh root ginger, and the reduced carrot juice. Bring to a boil and season. Purée in a blender. If you want a really smooth texture, pass through a sieve

RECIPE // MELLOW MISO BROTH CUBES

> Bring 500ml (16 fl oz) white miso broth, 225g (8oz) sweetcorn pulp (mashed kernels), 240ml (8 fl oz) white vegetable stock, and 240ml (8 fl oz) rice milk to a boil with 2 tbsp minced pickled ginger, 1 tbsp minced garlic, and 1 tsp cayenne. Reduce until thick enough to coat the back of a spoon. Purée (or not, if you enjoy texture). Add 60g (2oz) minced, sautéed shiitake mushrooms and 3 tbsp minced fresh chives.

RECIPE // TOMATO-BASIL CUBES

> Slowly cook 2 super-fresh garlic cloves, sliced really thin, in 3 tbsp olive oil, without browning, until the garlic has melted into the oil. Add 2 tbsp red wine vinegar and let mingle, then add 1 tsp sugar. After a little bubble action, cool it down with crushed tomato pulp (4 or 5 good heirloom tomatoes, vine-ripes, or Romas passed through the mincer attachment of an electric mixer) and 2 cans good organic vegetable juice. Bring to a boil. Stir in the picked leaves from a bunch of basil. Purée or leave chunky.

FREEZING PASTA SAUCES, SOUPS, AND STOCK

//
> Only a fool would make a single serving of pasta sauce or soup. Always make a big full pot, and freeze the leftovers in useful-size containers.
> Soups hold up really well after freezing and reheating. They come back to life beautifully. To freeze soup, cool it gradually in the fridge and then transfer it to the freezer. Before freezing, make sure to wipe any condensation from the outside of the container.
> I like to freeze soup in smallish containers, for individual servings of instant gratification. You can even take these directly from the freezer to work with you, and reheat them at lunch time.
> After you make a roast chicken, freeze up the leftover skin and bones in a bag to make a quick chicken stock kit for later. You can even freeze up the carrot sticks, sliced onion, and celery in advance, so when you want to make the stock, all you have left to do is season, add water, and boil!
//

THE 3 WAYS I FREEZE STOCK
//
> In ice cube trays for quick-hit flavour infusions to sauces and meat dishes.
> In handy containers for use in recipes that call for stock.
> In 1-litre (1 pint) containers for use as a base for new soups.
//

RECIPE // COOL AND SPICY TOMATO SOUP

> Pulp 4 peeled and seeded nice-size tomatoes (pass through the grinder attachment of an electric mixer), followed by half a small peeled, seeded cucumber and 1 serrano or jalapeño chilli (seeded). Soften 1 minced shallot in 4 tbsp olive oil. Add the vegetable pulp along with 2 tbsp Banyuls vinegar and 1 tsp freshly ground cumin. Bring just to a boil. Purée in a blender until super-ultra-smooth (or leave it chunky). Pour into freezer container(s), cool, and freeze for up to 3 months.

To serve, thaw the soup and season. For each portion, purée a small handful of rocket with 1 tbsp vegetable stock and ¼ tsp lemon juice until smooth – not too long or the heat from the motor will turn your rocket black. Serve the soup garnished with the puréed rocket in the centre, a drizzle of extra virgin olive oil, and shaved Parmesan. Serves 4

RECIPE // CARAMELIZED MUSHROOM SAUCE

> Sauté 900g (2lb) portobello mushrooms, sliced medium-thick, in 60ml (2 fl oz) olive oil with a seasoning of pepper. Once they're golden brown, add 2 small shallots and 1 small white part of leek (all minced) and cook until translucent. Add 1 tsp smoked Spanish paprika, a small pinch of celery seed, 1 tsp ground cumin, ½ tsp ground fennel, and 1 tbsp grated orange zest, followed by 115ml (4 fl oz) sherry vinegar. Stir well, then reduce until almost dry. Add 3l (5¼ pints) good, strong, clear chicken or vegetable stock. Bring to a boil, then simmer to reduce by two-thirds. Strain. Pour into freezer containers, cool, and freeze for up to 3 months.

Reheat to serve, then taste and season. Whisk in 1 tbsp chilled butter for the French effect or olive oil to go Mediterranean. This sauce goes really well with roasted pork, chicken, turkey, or lamb. Makes about 2l (3½ pints)

THE 3 STEPS TO WRAPPING MEATS AND FISH FOR THE FREEZER

1 WRAP THE ITEM IN PLASTIC WRAP, THEN WHITE BUTCHER PAPER OR ALUMINIUM FOIL

2 LABEL CLEARLY WHAT IS INSIDE AND DATE IT

3 SEAL THE PACKAGE IN AN AIRTIGHT BAG, SQUEEZING OUT ALL THE EXCESS SO NO AIR POCKETS REMAIN: AIR CONTAINS MOISTURE, WHICH TURNS TO FROST

FREEZING MEAT AND FISH

//

> When you take the time to go to a good butcher or fishmonger, it makes sense to buy in bulk so you can freeze individual-sized portions for later. This is where a vacuum sealer is particularly useful, but a high-quality locking freezer bag will work fine, too.

> Time-saver: When you make a tasty marinade, whip up an extra batch and toss it in a freezer bag with some fresh meat, fish, or poultry to freeze for another day. By the time the meat has thawed for cooking, it has been marinated, too.

> I'm known to hoard things when I find something great in season. This is especially true for wild salmon. In a good tight-sealed package, it will keep for six months in the freezer. But in my house, it's always gone before that.

> Artisanal sausages (made fresh without sodium nitrate and sodium nitrite, and other unnatural preservatives) are ideal to keep in the freezer. They thaw quickly, and a good sliced sausage or two can elevate soups, pastas, omelettes, and frittatas to hearty, full-meal status. They're also great to throw on the grill or pan-fry for a quick delicious sandwich. For added convenience and good health, look for low-fat sausages that have been smoked or precooked, so you can safely add them to your soup or pasta with just a quick reheat.

> Always thaw meat, poultry, fish, and seafood in the fridge to make sure they stay fresh. This means you will need to remember to transfer them from the freezer to the fridge a day or two before you want to use them. Meats that are still partly frozen when cooked develop a rubbery consistency.

> Keep in mind that at the supermarket, a lot of the fish, poultry, and meat has been previously frozen and thawed – especially seafood. Make sure you know what you're buying, and if something has already been frozen, don't refreeze it (unless you cook it first).

//

OUR REFRIGERATORS, OURSELVES

// YOUR REFRIGERATOR IS WHAT'S GOING TO MAKE OR BREAK YOU AS FAR AS BEING ABLE TO EAT WELL GOES. IN MY FRIDGE, THERE ARE MORE CONDIMENTS THAN ANYTHING ELSE. THEY TAKE UP A WHOLE SHELF OF THEIR OWN. BUT WHEN IT COMES TO EATING CLEAN ON THE FLY, THERE'S NOTHING MORE IMPORTANT THAN A FRIDGE STOCKED WITH WHATEVER IS FRESH AND IN SEASON.

THE SALAD DRAWER

// When you have a salad in the fridge drawer all washed and ready to go, you can literally grab a handful of clean greens right out of the fridge. Now there's absolutely no excuse for failing to include a salad with your meal. I also keep a steady supply of cabbage, broccoli, cucumber, and bell peppers in the drawer all the time, too.

THE BEST WAY TO MAKE SURE YOU EAT YOUR RAW GREENS
///
> Buy the greens prewashed, and wash them again when you get home
from the market. Wholehead greens are good too, but they will require
more advance work.
> Rinse your greens aggressively in cold water. Spin them dry in a salad
spinner, and store them in your salad drawer in a clean sealed container.
(I suggest you simply save a few of those plastic containers from the
supermarket and reuse them again and again.)
> You don't want to keep your greens sitting around in the fridge for more
than a week; they become limp and unappetizing. So eat them up!
///

CARROTS FOR SNACKING
// Those prepeeled baby carrots are a fine convenience item, but they
get white and scaly if you don't take good care of them. To keep them fresh
and crisp, remove them from the original bag, rinse well, and store in a
sealed container with a few teaspoons of fresh water. This will help retain
their colour and crispness. If you want a fuller-flavour carrot, buy medium-
sized carrots by the bunch at your local farmers' market, peel them, and
store them the same way for a quick crudité.

TOMATOES. DON'T REFRIGERATE
// An important exception to my refrigerator storage rule is tomatoes.
I always store them on the countertop instead of in the fridge. They
maintain their natural sweetness this way, and I think they actually
taste better at room temperature.

MILK. IT'S WHOLE FOR ME

// Health establishments will disagree, but I'm a whole milk guy. I like my milk to taste like milk, and I think whole-milk yogurt is hearty, beneficial, and satisfying. In my mind, whole foods of any kind – the way they occur in nature – are better for your body than scientifically engineered, processed, fat-reduced food byproducts. That goes for milk, too.

// Watching your fat intake? Pick your evil. I would much rather drink a glass of whole milk, or have a great yogurt parfait, than wolf down a couple of cheeseburgers. Of course, if you have particular medical reasons for maintaining a low-fat diet, please consider your own health above my personal preferences!

// Organic milk is best. Second-best is milk that comes from cows not treated with the hormone rBST, which boosts milk production. If a milk is rBST-free, it will be clearly labelled. Otherwise, you can be pretty sure the cow was on hormones when she made your milk.

NOT FROM THE COW

// If you have problems digesting dairy products and need a substitute, or if you're cooking for someone who does, I prefer rice milk over soya milk. Soya milk tastes chalky. Rice milk has a cleaner finish.

EGGS. ONLY THE BEST

// For health and humanitarian reasons, I only buy eggs from cage-free chickens. Eggs from cage-free chickens that were fed flax seed in their diet are even better, because that means the eggs have more healthy Omega-3 fatty acids.

IT'S WORTH CROSSING THE ROAD FOR HIGH-QUALITY EGGS.

YOGURT. I LOVE IT

///

> Always keep some plain, organic yogurt in the refrigerator. It's great
for cooking, but even better for eating.
> I eat yogurt plain or I flavour it with fresh fruit, preserves, or fruit
concentrates.
> The live cultures in fresh yogurt help your body to digest food efficiently,
and serve to maintain the colonies of healthy bacteria that live in your
intestinal track.
> Look for organic yogurt, from a local dairy if possible, made with whole
milk. Check the label to make sure it has several live cultures.
> Yogurt is a good breakfast or snack food, and it makes a lovely dessert
layered with beautiful fruits and nuts and drizzled with honey.
> Yogurt and seasonings make a great topping for baked fish or poultry
(see my recipe on page 206), and a fresh, light base for sauces.

///

YOGURT IS AN IDEAL CHOICE FOR QUICK, HEALTHY EATING.

CHEESE, PLEASE!

// When it comes to cheese, I recommend small quantities of high quality. There are good mainstream cheeses available on the market, but there's a lot of junk out there, too. Don't waste your calories on bad cheese. Save up for the good stuff, and have a couple of bites with a glass of wine while you're making dinner or checking emails. Or serve a cheese plate to finish a special dinner for your friends.

// After my dinner guests go home, I don't throw out the little odds and ends left over on the cheese plate. I put them all into a sealed tub in the fridge. When I have enough little bites saved up, I cut off any blue fuzzy parts and make a batch of my mystery fondue. (Don't use extra firm cheeses for this, only the soft ones with a good melting quality.) I like to melt a pan of fondue for Kimmie and me to enjoy while I'm working on something in the kitchen. That way she'll stay and read the paper, and keep me company.

RECIPE // MYSTERY FONDUE

> Sauté some chopped shallots and garlic in a small saucepan. Toss in whatever herbs or spices take your fancy (I like dried mustard seed). Add 500ml (1 pint) white wine – depending on how much cheese you have – and simmer until it reduces by half. Throw in the cheese and stir until it's smooth and creamy. Slice up a handful of bread cubes for dipping, and you've got yourself a snack.

FRESH FROM THE SEA

// There should regularly be fresh, wild-caught fish in your fridge, but never kept for more than a day or so. Fish should be purchased as close as possible to the day you intend to prepare it. If you can't cook it right away, or if you find a great deal on fresh fish in the market, freeze it in a tightly sealed bag for later.

// I never buy farm-raised fish because I think it causes a great deal of pollution, and can contain unseemly levels of pollutants. Rather, I prefer to buy what's available fresh and locally. When the discount warehouse store in my neighbourhood is selling fresh, wild-caught Copper River salmon, I buy them out and seal it up in smaller quantities for the freezer.

// If I'm going to freeze a large piece of salmon that I know is destined for the wood-burning grill, I season it up in advance. (Every little step counts in a busy day!) Then all I have to think about before we actually eat it is what to serve along with it.

// Truly fresh seafood is hard to find. Most of the prawns and scallops available on the market are previously frozen. It's okay to buy them frozen and keep in the freezer. Thaw seafood on the day you're going to use it, and rinse it thoroughly with cold running water in a colander.

EAT ONLY WHAT WE CAN TAKE FROM THE SEA IN GOOD CONSCIENCE.

BE A RESPONSIBLE FISH CONSUMER

// It's critically important to take responsibility for the consequences of what we take from the sea. As developing nations become wealthier, and as the health benefits of consuming fish become more widely understood, the world's appetite for fish is skyrocketing. We have to learn to wait our turn, and eat only what we can take from the sea in good conscience, or soon there will literally be nothing left.

// Be a nosy, scrupulous fish consumer. Ask hard questions, and be willing to walk away if you don't find something that meets your standards. I don't buy any seafood that doesn't meet the sustainable fishing guidelines, and you shouldn't either (see page 255).

"UNCURED" DELI MEATS

// The preservatives sodium nitrate and sodium nitrite are big no-no's in my book, so those highly processed sandwich meats you grew up on are officially off-limits. But that doesn't mean you can't have a good turkey or salami sandwich when the urge strikes you.

// An increasing number of sustainable-farmed, "uncured" (or "naturally cured") deli meats are available now, many using celery juice as a natural, healthy preservative. You can find them at health food shops and some of the more health-conscious chain stores, including Whole Foods. Their shelf-life is much shorter than processed lunch meats, but then again, they taste better so you won't mind eating them up quickly. They're not going to last for two months in your fridge, but you're not going to damage your health either. It's an easy trade-off, if you ask me.

// If you can't find "uncured" turkey, ham, roast beef, salami, hot dogs, bacon, or turkey bacon at your local stores, they are worth asking for. You just might be the one who tips the scales and encourages your shopkeepers to make some new, healthy choices available for the whole community to try out and enjoy.

// When I was cooking for Google, Larry loved a good fast-food sandwich from Subway, so I had to come up with lunch meats that tasted like they were processed, but weren't. In those days I had to be pretty aggressive to find "uncured" deli meats, but today they are much easier to find.

CONDIMENTS

// I have more condiments in my fridge than anything else. I think condiments should be no exception to smart eating. Be conscious of what ingredients are in there, and what your threshold is for buying rubbish.

MY FAVOURITE CONDIMENTS
//

> **Miso paste**. I use light-coloured miso pastes in spring and summer months, and red and dark-coloured misos in the winter and autumn. They are great as a liquid base for vegetarian soups or sauces. Use about 1 tsp per 230ml (8 fl oz).
> **Fermented dry black beans**.
> **Truffle oil and truffle butter**.
> **Indian chutneys**. I really like Indian-style mango chutney. I mix it with Dijon mustard as a spread for chicken sandwiches. It works well in chicken salad that way as well.
> **Japanese mayo**. My favourite, most versatile "secret sauce" is a sweet Japanese mayonnaise in a squeezy bottle called Kewpie. It was my best spread in the panini bar at Google. Spread on the outside of the bread instead of butter, it made for a deliciously crisp toasted sandwich.
> **Tartar sauce**.
> **Cocktail sauce**.
> **Mustard**. Lots of different mustards.
> **Ketchup**. I know some people who will make their own ketchup, but come on. Ketchup is out there. It's been proven. Spend your time on other things.
//

MAYONNAISE

// I learned to appreciate mayonnaise at this diner where I used to work in Rhode Island. The owner would rip off the label from a huge tub of mayonnaise, and transfer the contents into containers that were labelled "spread", so no one would realize he was just putting mayonnaise on everything. We used it in the frying pan to make the crispest, most delicious grilled cheese sandwiches in town. I don't use regular mass-market mayonnaise anymore; I prefer the Japanese mayonnaise from a smaller producer that has cleaner practices and ingredients.

MY NAME IS CHARLIE AND I USE KETCHUP

// Don't go thinking that "special red sauce #1" is your primary source of essential vitamins and nutrients. It certainly is not meant to replace eating tomatoes, and cannot be counted as a vegetable – contrary to what our son, Chance, claims. But there is no shame in reaching for the ketchup bottle. There are some wonderful organic ketchups out there now.

HOMEMADE CONDIMENTS

RECIPE // CHUTNEY-YOGURT CRUST
> Mix mango chutney to taste with plain yogurt and a little turmeric. Coat some salmon in that, cover it, and let it sit in the fridge for a couple of hours. Then grill it. The chutney-yogurt mix browns up nicely – like a toasted marshmallow – and makes a really good crust.

RECIPE // CRUSTY MISO GLAZE
> Blend miso paste in the food processor with a little bit of sake, toasted sesame oil, and Dijon mustard, or ginger and garlic. Spoon it over fish, let it marinate for a day, and then grill it. If you want some heat, use red miso paste and put a little cayenne in there too. If you're using white miso, try adding a pinch of ground coriander or cumin. Serve the fish with minced spring onion and steamed brown rice.

RECIPE // JAPANESE MAYO COATING
> Stir sweet Japanese mayonnaise with a little bit of miso paste and wasabi powder, and spread over fish or chicken before grilling.

RECIPE // KETCHUP GLAZE
> Flavour organic ketchup with a small amount of Chinese five-spice, dry sherry, and tamari, and you have a kick-ass glaze to put over salmon that is being grilled.

RECIPE // ROASTED JALAPEÑO KETCHUP
> Roast the hell out of some jalapeños, then skin and seed them. Put into a blender, add some orange juice, ground cumin, and ketchup, and purée. Transfer to a container and keep refrigerated.

CURRY PASTES AND FISH SAUCE

// I have fallen in love with the complicated flavour profiles you can find in ready-made curry pastes. Unlike the dry powders commonly used in India, Pakistan, and Sri Lanka, wet pastes are used in the cooking from Japan, Thailand, and Malaysia. In addition to the usual curry spices, pastes often include fish sauce, root ginger, galangal root, or citrus juices. They come in jars, tubes, or little buckets and have a long shelf life, but should be refrigerated after opening.

// Fish sauce is a great way to up the flavour profile of a lot of dishes. It can do wonders for a marinade or glaze for meat, poultry, or seafood, or can finish off a stir-fry. I started using fish sauce even in non-Asian dishes after realizing it was anchovies that made plain old Worcestershire sauce so tasty. Now I shop around, tasting a lot of different fish sauces, because it helps deepen my dishes, giving them that full-mouth flavour known in Japanese philosophy as "umami", or the fifth taste. It's that feeling of well-being and satisfaction we find in things like chocolate, wine, and certain coffees. I think there's definitely a sense of well-being to be found in the right fish sauce. I particularly like the Three Crabs brand of fish sauce, which is a product from Thailand that is manufactured in Vietnam.

// Before using fish sauce, be conscious of who you're feeding. Vegetarians and people with seafood allergies should not be served fish sauce.

HOW TO ASK FOR FISH SAUCE
//
> In Vietnam, it's called "nuoc mam".
> In Thailand, they call it "nam pla".
> In the Philippines, ask for "patis".
//

STOCK UP ON STOCK

// I keep jars of homemade highly concentrated stock in my refrigerator. If you have time to spend the day properly reducing a hearty beef or chicken stock, you will reap the dividends for a long time to come. Called a "glace de vien," it's a concentrate that should be as dense as shoe polish. Use it a tablespoon at a time to bring full, yummy flavours to your soups, sauces, stir-frys, and grains. Stored in a clean, airtight jar in the fridge, it should be good for several months. It can also be frozen in ice cube trays.

RECIPE // GLACE DE VIEN

> Mince up 4 shallots and put in a pan with 1 tsp black peppercorns, 2 bay leaves, and 2 sprigs of thyme. Pour in ¼ bottle of good bourbon and boil until almost dry. Then add ½ bottle of port wine, and reduce that until it's almost dry. It will have a very sticky consistency. Add 1l (1³/4 pints of good, reduced, homemade beef stock and cook at a very low simmer for about 1 hour. Strain and continue to reduce in a small pan until syrupy. Pour into a small container for storage.

STORE UP SOME HERB SALT

// I like to make a big batch of this bright green herb salt at a time, then keep a small container on the countertop and refrigerate the rest in an airtight container for later.

// My herb salt is great to use at the end of cooking for sauces, and in mashed potatoes, stuffing, and soups. It gives an added punch to almost any really savoury dish. I always add it right at the end so the fresh herb flavour is not cooked out. I steer away from using it in Asian-inspired dishes because it really muddles up those flavours.

RECIPE // HERB SALT

> Pick the leaves from a large sprig each of fresh thyme, oregano, and sage. Grind with 230g (8oz) kosher salt and 2 peeled garlic cloves to make a paste. It will be bright green. Mix with 1 tsp each freshly grated nutmeg and white pepper. Work through large-hole chinoise strainer, if needed.

MORE KITCHEN ESSENTIALS

// FOR ME, THE FOODS YOU SHOULD HAVE ON HAND TO MAKE LIFE WORTH LIVING ARE GOOD BREAD, GOOD BEER, AND CHOCOLATE. GROWING SOME OF YOUR OWN FOOD IS ANOTHER ESSENTIAL TO AIM FOR — EVEN IF IT'S ONLY SOME HERBS ON A WINDOWSILL. AND OF COURSE GOOD KITCHEN TOOLS ARE WHAT MAKE COOKING A PLEASURE.

GOOD BREAD IS A MUST

// Like cheese, you should be willing to sacrifice quantity for quality in your diet. If you're going to eat bread, it should be handcrafted, wholegrain, and delicious. Buy a good bread without preservatives, and freeze half or two-thirds of it for later. That way, it won't get stale and you can continue to enjoy it for a few more days.

RECYCLE YOUR BREAD

// Don't throw out the odds and ends of bread. A lot of good crusty bread in my house ends up in a bag in the freezer. When I have enough, I dice it up and make croûtons under the grill. Sometimes the croûtons end up on a salad, sometimes they become stuffing. And sometimes they get thrown in the food processor and chopped into high-quality bread crumbs. The bread crumbs can be frozen again in small sealed bags.

BEER IS A HAPPINESS ITEM

// I'm not willing to give up beer. But I only buy local, handcrafted beer. If it's organic, even better. Most communities have their own locally handcrafted beers. And even some decent local wines are available in unexpected parts of the country. I recently tasted a pleasant wine from Wisconsin. Make the effort to find what's brewing in your region. You might be happily surprised.

CHOCOLATE IS A NON-NEGOTIABLE PART OF MY LIFE

// Okay, so they don't grow cocoa beans in California, but our carbon footprints aside, you and I both know that we've gotta have chocolate. Where I live, we are lucky to have several outstanding local artisanal chocolatemakers to choose from. The beans come from far away, but the distribution is local.

IN SMALL AMOUNTS, THE CAFFEINE IN COCOA BEANS CAN STIMULATE YOUR MIND AND HELP YOU FOCUS.

4 BEST HERBS TO GROW AT HOME
1 CHIVES 2 BASIL

3 PARSLEY 4 MINT

GROW IT YOURSELF

// **There is nothing more satisfying than cooking with food you have grown yourself. Whether it's a patch of lettuce in your garden or a little box of fresh parsley and chives growing in your window, your spirits and your dishes will be elevated if you can grow some of your food at home.**

// Most common herbs are relatively easy to grow, and taste all the better when they are used fresh off the plant. Oregano tastes really good fresh, but it's not a quick grower. Check your local nursery to see what herbs will do well in your climate.

// The best veggies to grow yourself are salad leaves and tomatoes, if your local climate allows. Homegrown tomatoes are SO much better than shop-bought that they are no doubt worth the effort.

// I don't have much room for gardening at home, so this year I'm growing my own cherry tomatoes in my kitchen with a hydroponic countertop grower. This really works and the tomatoes taste great.

MUST-HAVE EXTRA TOOLS

//
> Rice cooker
> Slow cooker
> Coffee grinders for spices (I have three coffee grinders: one for coffee, one for spices, and one for hot chillies)
> Food processor
> Hand or immersion blender
//

THE EASIEST MEAL EVER

// A slow cooker is one of the best time-savers in the kitchen. I use mine for cooking short ribs, stews, chilli, and shanks, and for those large, hearty, inexpensive cuts of meat that take a long time to soften up. There's no need to go all Julia Child over those meats with a day's worth of braising and the big bunch of fuss. Just sear the meat in the morning, put it in the slow cooker, and throw in some herbs, onions, and celery. Add a little boiling stock or other liquid (about half the amount you would normally add) and let the meat cook on low heat all day. When you come home, the house will smell great and your dinner will be ready.

A MANDOLIN SLICER FOR GARLIC

// If you want to buy yourself a present, I think a Japanese mandolin slicer is a great extra tool to have. I hate peeling a clove of garlic and putting it on the cutting board to slice it, because it stinks up the board and the knife and my fingers. I can put my little mandolin slicer right over whatever I'm cooking, and cut the garlic right into the pan. If I were making a sauce, and didn't want the look of garlic slices, I would use a garlic press instead of the mandolin.

SAVE YOUR CONTAINERS, SAVE THE EARTH

// Recycling is a game in my house. We're always trying to ask ourselves: How can we reuse this? If we can't reuse it, we recycle it. When a food product comes swaddled in a lot of nonrecyclable packaging, your best choice is not to buy it.

// I am a big fan of recycled jars and plastic containers for my storage needs, particularly in the freezer. Just make sure they're dishwasher-clean before you reuse them. And always label the contents clearly with an indelible marker so you can tell what's in there without opening the container and exposing it to potential freezer burn.

// I think plastic is fine for storage purposes, but I don't ever reheat my food in plastic containers. The recycled tubs may not have been specifically engineered for high temperatures, and you never know when something might leak chemicals into your food when heated. Remove frozen food from the plastic container – run hot water along the outside of the container – and slide into a glass, metal, or earthenware dish. Or, thaw in the fridge until the food can be poured into a pot for reheating.

NO NUKES, PLEASE!

// I recommend not using a microwave oven. I believe in heating my food the old-fashioned way. I know you're busy, but be smart about your kitchen time. Pour yourself a glass of wine, and take that time while your food reheats to check your email, read the newspaper, plan tomorrow's dinner, or call a friend.

EVERYTHING IN MODERATION

// In the early days, Google did have a tendency to smell like a frat house. Those engineers never went home. There were piles of laundry strewn about, and mats all over the floor. I used to think they had a lot of pets there because of all those mats, but it turned out that's where they were sleeping. The engineers would play roller hockey out in the car park, and then come rolling into my café all sweaty and dirty with their trays out for a meal. Once Google was able to hire some women, the guys finally started showering. That's when the place started to run more smoothly, too.

// There was this one Googler named Lori Park. She was a mouthy girl from Harvard, and we were good friends. Lori was the one who got them to start printing up some women's t-shirts at Google. They had t-shirts for everything there. She's also the one who got me to cut back on the big meat and potato menus. At Lori's urging, I started offering a more diverse menu with a lot of salads, and I opened a panini bar. Both were really popular, but it backfired in a way. People weren't eating salads instead of the big hearty meals I had cooked. A lot of them were eating the big hearty meals I cooked and having a sandwich or a salad on top of it.

// Well, wouldn't you know it, some people got fat. (Vast quantities of delicious, expensive food, lovingly prepared by an innovative chef, available free of charge, will have a tendency to do that to you!) So they hired a bunch of boot camp instructors to make them run around the car park in order to squeeze back into their cubicles. I wasn't supposed to know this, but the fat camp instructors were wearing t-shirts emblazoned with a red slash through a picture of my face. I thought it was funny, but I told them the same thing I'll tell you: It's not my fault.

// Food is good. Good, healthy food is even better. But we all know that too much food can kill you. Meanwhile, everything tastes better with a lot of fresh air and exercise. So walk to the shops. Take the stairs. Run around the car park if you have to. And put back that panini if you've already had lunch!

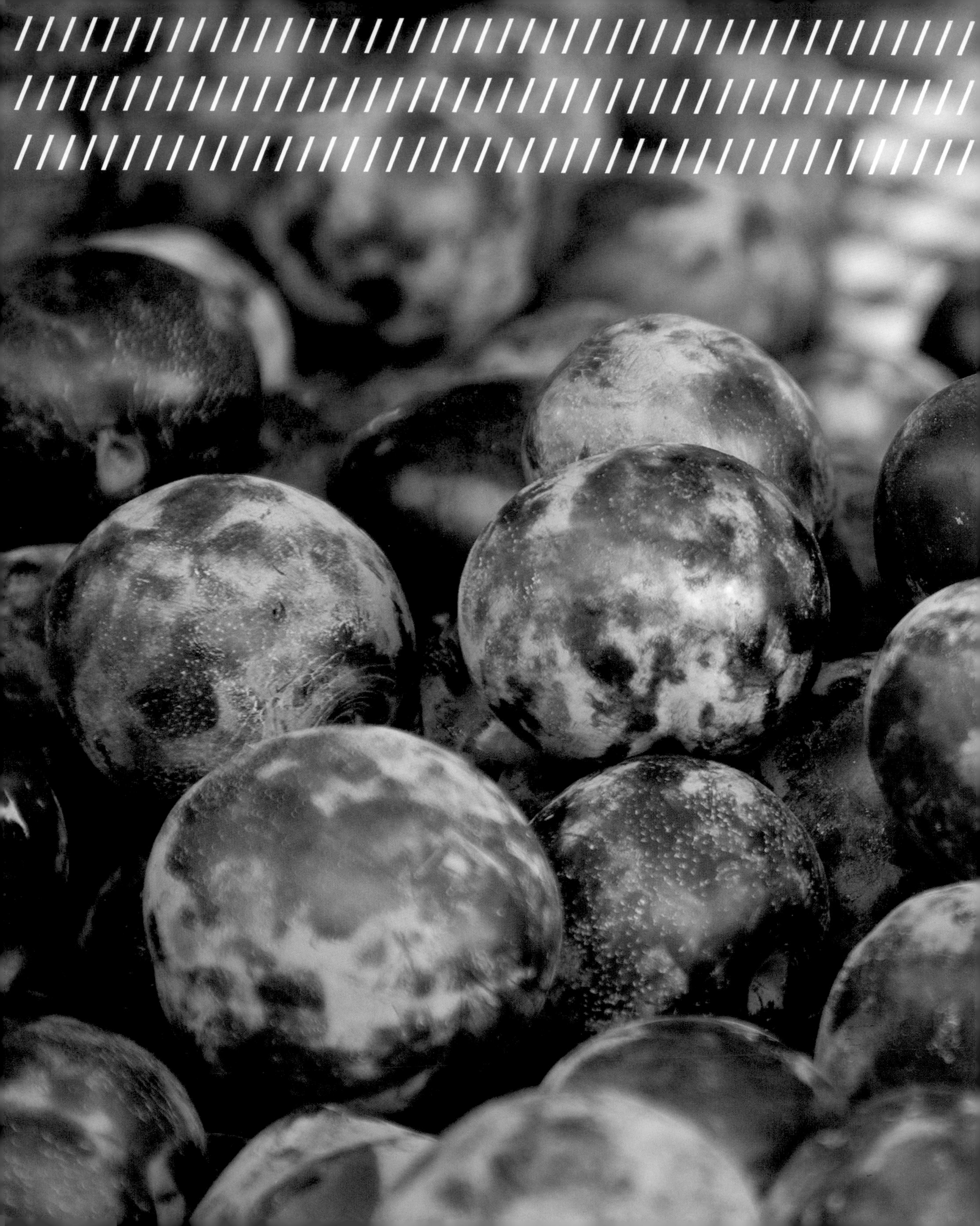

SMART RECIPES

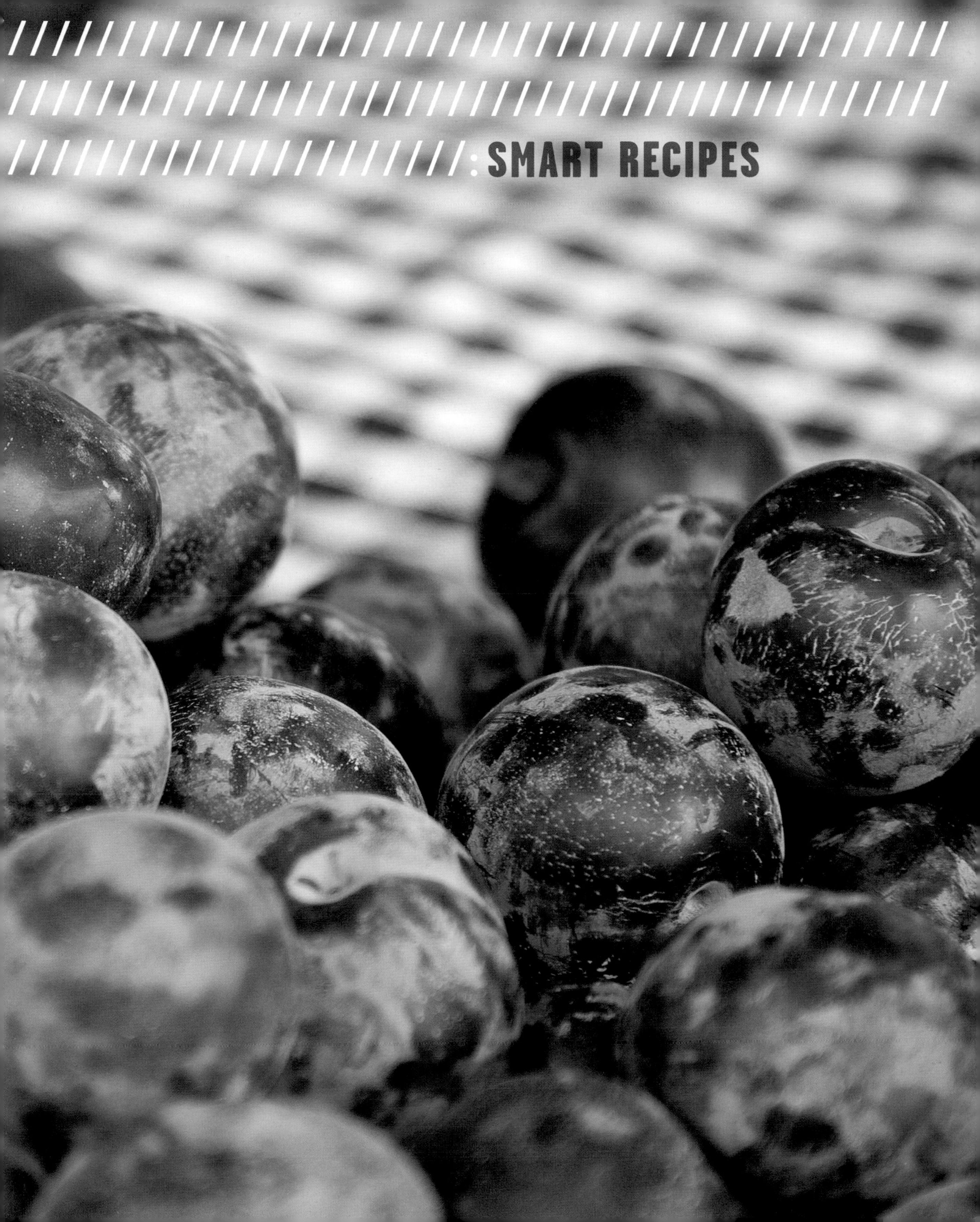

START MY DAY

SET THE COURSE OF YOUR DAY BY STARTING IT RIGHT. IF YOU KNOW YOU'LL BE BUSY AND WANT TO POWER UP, OPT FOR WHOLEGRAINS, YOGURT, FRESH FRUIT, AND GREEN TEA RATHER THAN SAUSAGE, EGGS, AND COFFEE. CONSIDER BREAKFAST AN INVESTMENT IN YOUR DAY. IF YOU ONLY HAVE COFFEE, YOU'RE NOT HELPING ANYONE EXCEPT THE GUY WHO SOLD YOU THE COFFEE.

BLACK AND BLUE YOGURT FRU FRU >>

SERVES 1 /// PREP TIME: 6 MINUTES /// COOK TIME: 0

1 tbsp toasted flaked almonds
2 tsp orange-blossom mountain honey
30g (1oz) blueberries
120ml (4fl oz) Greek-style yogurt
30g (1oz) blackberries
¼ tsp ground cinnamon

> Put the toasted almonds at the bottom of a sundae glass and drizzle
1 tsp of the honey over them. Put the blueberries on top and then half the
yogurt. Spoon in the blackberries and then the remaining yogurt. Drizzle
with the rest of the honey and dust with cinnamon. Chill overnight, and
enjoy first thing in the morning.

// This dish looks best served in a sundae glass and made the night before
you want to eat it.

DREAMY PEACH SMOOTHIE

SERVES 1 /// PREP TIME: 5 MINUTES /// COOK TIME: 0

1 peach, stoned and diced
4 large strawberries, hulled
1 banana, cut into pieces
Good pinch of ground cinnamon
250ml (8fl oz) thick vanilla yogurt
Handful of crushed ice
Small fresh mint sprig for garnish

> Put all the ingredients into a blender. Blend until thick and smooth.
Pour into a glass, garnish with a small mint sprig, and serve.

CITRUS CRUSHER

SERVES 4 /// PREP TIME: 5 MINUTES /// COOK TIME: 0
500ml (16fl oz) fresh ruby red or pink grapefruit juice
250ml (8fl oz) pineapple juice
250ml (8fl oz) fresh orange juice
Lime-flavoured sparkling mineral water, chilled

> Prepare this the night before you want to drink it. Fill 12 sections
of an ice cube tray with some of the grapefruit juice and freeze.

> Mix the pineapple, orange, and remaining grapefruit juices together
and chill for several hours or overnight.

> When ready to serve, put three frozen cubes of grapefruit juice in
each of four large glasses. Pour on the mixed juices, fill the glasses
with sparkling lime-flavoured water, and stir. Drink through a straw.

// With all smoothie recipes, it is best to use freshly squeezed juices
whenever possible. This smoothie can be spiked with vodka or gin,
to make a great brunch party drink.

HAWAIIAN KITCHEN-SINK SMOOTHIE

SERVES 4 /// PREP TIME: 10 MINUTES /// COOK TIME: 0

4 bananas, cut in pieces
120ml (4fl oz) fresh orange juice
60ml (2fl oz) apple juice
225g (8oz) can pineapple in natural juice
60g (2oz) fresh or frozen blueberries
10–12 fresh or frozen strawberries
250ml (8fl oz) pineapple juice
400g (14oz) can coconut milk, chilled
250ml (8fl oz) plain yogurt
2 tbsp fresh lemon juice
4 tsp orange-blossom honey (optional)
12 ice cubes
4 small, fresh strawberries for garnish (optional)

> Put all the ingredients, except the ice cubes, in a blender, adding the honey if you want a slightly sweeter smoothie. Blend until smooth, dropping in the ice cubes a few at a time.

> Pour into glasses. If garnishing, make a small slit in each strawberry and push one onto the rim of each glass. Serve immediately.

// I make this for four people so I use the whole can of coconut milk and the can of pineapple. But you can make less, and keep the rest of the coconut milk and fruit in the fridge for another smoothie (use them up within a day or two).

JADE SMOOTHIE

SERVES 1 /// PREP TIME: 5 MINUTES /// COOK TIME: 0
¼–½ cucumber
6 large, fresh mint leaves
120ml (4fl oz) apple juice
4 tbsp lemon sorbet
4 ice cubes

> Cut a slice off the cucumber and reserve for garnish. Peel the cucumber and split it lengthwise, then scoop out the seeds with a teaspoon. Roughly chop the cucumber.

> Place in a blender with the remaining ingredients. Blend until smooth. Pour into a glass, garnish with the halved cucumber slice, and serve.

IF YOU DON'T HAVE TIME TO EAT YOUR BREAKFAST THEN DRINK IT.

SCREWY RABBIT . . . THINK BRUNCH!

SERVES 2 /// PREP TIME: 5 MINUTES /// COOK TIME: 0

120ml (4fl oz) good vodka
120ml (4fl oz) fresh orange juice
250ml (8fl oz) fresh carrot juice
1 tbsp fresh lemon juice
2 washed baby carrots with the green tops intact (optional)

> Stir the vodka with the juices. Pour over ice in chilled highball glasses. Garnish each with a baby carrot if desired and serve.

// This is great for brunch or as an evening pick-me-up. I buy fresh carrot juice at the taquerias near my house so I don't have to go to the trouble and mess of making the juice myself.

THIS IS NOT ONE TO DRINK ON YOUR OWN OR FIRST THING IN THE MORNING.

<< SMOOTHIE SANDIA

SERVES 1 /// PREP TIME: 10 MINUTES /// COOK TIME: 0

Salt
85g (3oz) fresh or frozen blueberries, plus a few for garnish
120ml (4fl oz) pineapple juice
1 tsp wild-blossom honey
1 large wedge of watermelon, peeled, seeded, and cubed

> Dip the rim of a glass in water and then in bar salt. Thread a few blueberries on a toothpick or cocktail stick for garnish. Place the rest of the berries, the juice, honey, and watermelon in a blender, and mix on low speed until blended. Continue mixing, gradually increasing the speed, until smooth. Pour the smoothie into the glass and rest the stick of berries on the rim.

// There's nothing more refreshing than a watermelon smoothie when the temperature outside is rising faster than Google on a good day at the market. Add a shot of tequila to turn this into a relaxing evening cocktail.

PEACEFUL BERRY MORNING SMOOTHIE

SERVES 1 /// PREP TIME: 4 MINUTES /// COOK TIME: 0

1 banana, cut in pieces
60g (2oz) fresh or frozen strawberries
60g (2oz) fresh or frozen raspberries
120ml (4fl oz) thick strawberry yogurt
120ml (4fl oz) cranberry juice cocktail or apple juice –
   or you can even go for orange juice if you prefer

> Place all the ingredients in a blender. Blend until smooth. Serve.

WAKE-UP SHAKE-ME-UP POWER SHAKE >>

SERVES 1 /// PREP TIME: 8 MINUTES PLUS CHILLING /// COOK TIME: 0

120ml (4fl oz) strong-brewed black tea, chilled
120ml (4fl oz) rice milk
60ml (2fl oz) fresh orange juice
1 small banana, cut in pieces
1/4 cantaloupe melon, peeled, seeded, and diced
2 tsp wild-blossom honey
60g (2oz) fresh or frozen strawberries
An extra small sliver of melon for garnish

> Put all the ingredients in a blender. Blend until smooth. Pour into a large glass, garnish with a small sliver of melon on the rim, and serve.

// I often find smoothies to be a lot more invigorating and uplifting than a cup of coffee in the morning.

ORANGE CARROT CABARET

SERVES 1 /// PREP TIME: 10 MINUTES /// COOK TIME: 0

3 small ice cubes
2 apricots, stoned and sliced
1/2 papaya, peeled, stoned, and diced (or use frozen)
1/2 mango, peeled, stoned, and diced (or use frozen)
120ml (4fl oz) fresh carrot juice
1 tsp wild-blossom honey (optional)

> Put all the ingredients, except the honey, in a blender and blend until smooth. Taste and add the honey, if necessary, then blend for a few more seconds. Serve immediately in a frosted glass.

WASHINGTON NUTTY-BLUE SMOOTHIE

SERVES 1 /// PREP TIME: 5 MINUTES /// COOK TIME: 0

1 peach, stoned and sliced
60g (2 oz) fresh or frozen blueberries
250ml (8fl oz) vanilla yogurt, chilled
120ml (4fl oz) milk
½ tbsp smooth peanut butter
A pinch of kosher salt
¼ tsp natural vanilla extract
A few chopped raw peanuts for garnish (optional)

> Put all the ingredients into a blender and blend until smooth. Pour into a tall glass, garnish with a few chopped peanuts, if desired, and serve.

ALL-AROUND NUTRITIONAL SUPERSTARS, BLUEBERRIES CAN IMPROVE CONCENTRATION, SO STOCK UP.

WAKE-UP BREAKFAST SMOOTHIE

SERVES 1 /// PREP TIME: 15 MINUTES /// COOK TIME: 0

120ml (4fl oz) plain yogurt
120ml (4fl oz) fresh carrot juice
90ml (3fl oz) fresh orange juice
1 ripe banana, cut in pieces
30g (1oz) chopped melon
1 tsp pickled ginger
1 tbsp royal jelly (optional)
2 or 3 ice cubes

> Put all the ingredients in a blender and blend until smooth. Pour into
a tall glass and drink immediately.

MOUNT SHASTA FRUIT SMOOTHIE

SERVES 1 /// PREP TIME: 5 MINUTES /// COOK TIME: 0

1 nectarine or peach, stoned and sliced
1 banana, cut into pieces
2 tbsp wheatgerm
60ml (2fl oz) fresh orange juice
120ml (4fl oz) thick vanilla yogurt
2 or 3 ice cubes

> Reserve a slice of nectarine or peach and a pinch of wheat germ for
garnish, if desired. Put the remainder in a blender or food processor with
the rest of the ingredients. Blend until smooth.

> Pour into a tall glass, garnish with the reserved slice of fruit and pinch
of wheat germ, and serve.

« SMOOTHOCCINO

SERVES 1 /// PREP TIME: 5 MINUTES PLUS CHILLING /// COOK TIME: 0

250ml (8fl oz) brewed double-strength coffee, chilled
60ml (2fl oz) half fat cream, chilled
4 ice cubes
120ml (4fl oz) milk, chilled
Whipped cream (if you have company, or if you just want to treat yourself)
Ground cinnamon for garnish

> Put the coffee, half fat cream, ice cubes, and milk in a blender and blend until smooth and frothy. Pour into a glass coffee mug and add whipped cream, if feeling decadent. Dust with cinnamon before serving.

ZEN STRAWBERRY-ORANGE SMOOTHIE

SERVES 1 /// PREP TIME: 5 MINUTES PLUS CHILLING /// COOK TIME: 0

120ml (4fl oz) strong-brewed green tea, chilled
60g (2oz) sliced strawberries
120ml (4fl oz) fresh orange juice
Small handful of crushed ice
60ml (2fl oz) rice milk
1 tsp wild-blossom honey

> Put the tea in a blender. Reserve a few slices of strawberry for garnishing, if desired, and add the rest to the blender along with the remaining ingredients. Blend until smooth. Pour into a large glass. Garnish with the reserved sliced strawberries and serve.

FLUFFY SOYA PANCAKES

MAKES 8 /// PREP TIME: 10 MINUTES PLUS STANDING ///
COOK TIME: ABOUT 25 MINUTES

115g (4oz) unbleached all-purpose flour
60g (2oz) soya flour
2 tsp baking powder
1/4 tsp kosher salt
1 tbsp unrefined granulated sugar
2 eggs, separated
300ml (1/2 pint) milk
45g (1 1/2 oz) butter, melted
Canola oil

> Sift the flours with the baking powder and salt into a bowl. Beat the sugar and egg yolks together in another bowl until thick and pale. Gradually whisk in the milk and melted butter, and then the flour mixture, whisking well until smooth. Cover and let stand for 30 minutes.

> Beat the egg whites until stiff. Gently fold into the batter using a metal spoon, to retain the fluffiness of the egg whites.

> Heat a little oil in a frying pan. Pour off the excess, then add about 2 tbsp of the batter and spread out to make a 5in (12.5cm) pancake. Cook over medium heat until golden underneath and bubbles appear and burst on the surface. Flip over and cook the other side. Remove and keep warm in a low oven while you cook the remaining pancakes.

> Serve hot, with fruit-infused pancake syrup and icing sugar.

// Soya flour is another way of getting protein into your diet. You can eat these pancakes and skip the bacon.

APRICOT MULTIGRAIN BREAKFAST

MAKES ABOUT 1KG (2^{1}/2LB) CUPS /// PREP TIME: 5 MINUTES /// COOK TIME: 0

225g (8oz) rolled oats
225g (8oz) millet or barley flakes
115g (4oz) wheatgerm
60g (2oz) sesame seeds
60g (2oz) raw peanuts, roughly chopped
175g (6oz) raisins
175g (6oz) dried apricots, chopped
115g (4oz) dried banana slices, chopped if large
^{1}/4 tsp ground cinnamon
2 tsp finely chopped crystallized ginger
1 tbsp unrefined light brown sugar

> Mix all the ingredients together and store in an airtight container. Serve with milk and/or plain Greek-style yogurt and a trickle of honey, if desired.

// For a hot breakfast, mix equal parts cereal and milk in a saucepan. Bring to a boil, then reduce the heat and simmer gently, stirring occasionally, until thick and creamy, about 3 minutes. Serve as above.

GRAB & GO

GRANOLA

MAKES ABOUT 900G (2LB) /// PREP TIME: 5 MINUTES /// COOK TIME: 20 MINUTES

450g (1lb) rolled oats
60g (2oz) raw cashews
60g (2oz) sunflower seeds
115g (4oz) wheatgerm
60g (2oz) sesame seeds
60g (2oz) toasted hemp seeds
½ tsp kosher salt
85g (3oz) dried, unsweetened, flaked coconut (large)
60ml (2fl oz) canola oil
60ml (2fl oz) apple juice
4 tbsp orange-blossom honey
½ tsp natural vanilla extract

> Preheat the oven to 180°C (350°F/Gas 4). Mix all the dry ingredients together in a large mixing bowl. Mix all the wet ingredients together in a separate bowl, stirring until the honey has dissolved. Add to the dry ingredients and mix thoroughly.

> Spread evenly in two shallow baking tins. Bake until evenly golden brown, about 20 minutes, folding the browning granola from the edges into the centre of the tins with a metal spatula after every 5 minutes.

> Remove from the oven and tip into an airtight container. Leave until the granola is cold, then put on the lid to seal. Store in a cool, dry place. Serve with fresh fruit and plain yogurt.

THE ENGINEERS AT GOOGLE CALLED THIS CHARLIE'S MYSTICAL GRANOLA.

FRUITY SESAME-SEED GRANOLA

MAKES ABOUT 800G (1¾LB) /// PREP TIME: 5 MINUTES /// COOK TIME: 20 MINUTES

90ml (3fl oz) grapeseed oil
90ml (3fl oz) apple juice
4 tbsp wild-blossom honey
1½ tsp ground cinnamon
115g (4oz) rolled oats
115g (4oz) flaked almonds
115g (4oz) raw cashews
115g (4oz) dried, unsweetened, shredded coconut
85g (3oz) sesame seeds
125g (4½ oz) raisins
125g (4½ oz) moist dried cranberries or blueberries

> Preheat the oven to 180°C (350°F/Gas 4). Put the oil, apple cider, honey, and cinnamon in a large saucepan and bring to a boil, stirring. Stir in the oats, nuts, coconut, and seeds until everything is coated well.

> Spread the mixture evenly in two baking tins. Bake until golden brown, about 20 minutes, folding the browning granola from the edges into the center of the tins with a metal spatula after every 5 minutes.

> Stir in the raisins and cranberries or blueberries. Leave until completely cold before storing in an airtight container.

// This is much better than any store-bought granola. I eat it as dessert or carry it instead of gorp (trail mix) when backpacking. It is very good eaten straight, with no milk. If you choose to make it with blueberries, I'm sure you will love the granola mixed with a small amount of milk and smooth peanut butter. This makes a wonderful high-in-protein snack for early morning or late night.

CREAMY BREAKFAST POLENTA

SERVES 4 /// PREP TIME: 5 MINUTES /// COOK TIME: 4–11 MINUTES

250ml (8fl oz) single cream
600ml (1 pint) milk
Pinch of kosher salt
115g (4oz) coarse yellow cornmeal (polenta)
60g (2oz) unrefined light brown sugar, lightly packed
15g (½ oz) unsalted butter
½ tsp ground cinnamon
45g (1 ½ oz) currants or other dried berries
2 tbsp mascarpone or Neufchâtel cheese

> Combine the cream, milk, and salt in a heavy-based pan and bring almost to a boil. Add the cornmeal in a slow, steady stream, whisking constantly to keep the mixture smooth and free of lumps. Cook and whisk the mixture until it is thick, 3–10 minutes, adding more milk if the polenta becomes too thick. (Timing will vary depending on the cornmeal you use.) Stir in the brown sugar and butter with a wooden spoon and beat for 1 minute. Beat in the cinnamon and currants.

> Remove from the heat and beat in the mascarpone or Neufchâtel cheese. Serve immediately in individual bowls, with extra milk and some brown sugar, if desired.

// This takes a bit more time than porridge, but it's worth it, especially on cold, nasty mornings. It makes a delicious dessert, too.

POLENTA SETS A CALMING TONE FOR THE REST OF THE DAY.

BREAKFAST TACOS

SERVES 2 OR 4 /// PREP TIME: 15 MINUTES /// COOK TIME: 7 MINUTES

4 soft, yellow corn tortillas
15g (½ oz) butter
2 shallots, chopped
1 fresh, hot, red or green chilli (such as a Thai chilli), seeded and chopped
85g (3oz) cooked *carne asada* or leftover roast beef, shredded or chopped
6 dashes or so of your favourite hot sauce (see Google Hot Sauce, page 249)
60g (2oz) cooked long grain rice
2 eggs, beaten
Two good handfuls shredded green or Chinese cabbage or lettuce
Two good handfuls grated *queso fresco* or mozzarella cheese (optional)

> Warm the tortillas according to the package directions.

> Meanwhile, melt the butter in a nonstick frying pan and sauté the shallots until they are turning lightly golden, about 2 minutes. Add the chilli and meat, and stir until the meat is beginning to crisp a little. Hit it with the hot sauce, then add the rice and toss a couple times until the rice is hot throughout. Turn down the heat, add the eggs, and cook, stirring, until scrambled but not too dry.

> Remove from the heat and divide among the tortillas. Top with the shredded cabbage and then the cheese, if using. Roll up and eat.

// I came up with these when I was really hungover one morning. When I was grabbing the eggs I saw a leftover piece of steak next to them and I said, I have a place for you! If you don't have any leftover beef, quickly sauté a small frying steak, cut in thin shreds.

QUICK APPLE-OATY THING

SERVES 1 /// PREP TIME: 10 MINUTES /// COOK TIME: 5 MINUTES PLUS STANDING

85g (3oz) rolled oats
360ml (12fl oz) apple juice or water
1 small apple, cored and diced
2 tbsp of your favourite dried fruits, chopped if necessary
1 tbsp toasted pumpkin seeds
1 tbsp flaxseed oil
Wild-blossom honey
A large spoonful of thick plain or vanilla yogurt

> Combine the oats, apple cider or water, apple, dried fruits, and pumpkin seeds in a saucepan. Bring to a boil, then reduce the heat and simmer, stirring, until thick and the oats are cooked, about 5 minutes. The apple should still have some texture to it. Remove from the heat and let stand for 5 minutes.

> Stir in the flax oil and sweeten to taste with honey. Spoon into a serving bowl and top with the yogurt. Drizzle a little more honey over the top if you want a sweeter finish.

OATS ARE GREAT. THEY SLOW THE ABSORPTION OF GLUCOSE INTO THE BLOODSTREAM, GIVING YOU A STEADY RELEASE OF ENERGY.

CRANBERRY-ORANGE BREAD

MAKES 1 LOAF /// PREP TIME: 15 MINUTES /// COOK TIME: 1 1/4 HOURS

225g (8oz) fresh or thawed frozen cranberries
115g (4oz) unrefined granulated sugar
225g (8oz) unbleached all-purpose flour
60g (2oz) wholewheat flour
115g (4oz) unrefined light brown sugar, lightly packed
2 tsp baking powder
½ tsp bicarbonate of soda
½ tsp fine sea salt
Finely grated zest of 1 orange
Juice of 3 oranges
90ml (3fl oz) vegetable oil
1 egg
1 tsp natural vanilla extract
A little milk

> Preheat the oven to 180°C (350°F/Gas 4). Lightly oil a standard 23 by 12cm (9 by 5in) metal loaf tin. Dust the tin with flour and tap out the excess.

> Mix the cranberries and granulated sugar together in a small bowl. Set aside. In a separate bowl, mix the flours, brown sugar, baking powder, bicarbonate of soda, and salt. Set aside.

> Whisk together the orange zest, juice, oil, egg, and vanilla extract. Add to the flour mixture and stir just until the ingredients are barely combined. Fold in the sugared cranberries. Add a little milk, if needed, to make a soft consistency that will drop from the spoon when it is gently shaken. Transfer the batter to the prepared tin and level the surface.

> Bake until well risen, golden, and firm to the touch, about 1 ¼ hours. A skewer inserted in the centre should come out clean. Let cool until just warm, then run a knife around the inside of the pan and turn the loaf out onto a wire rack to cool completely. Serve sliced and buttered.

BEETROOT WITH BACON AND CRUMBLED BLUE CHEESE

SERVES 2 /// PREP TIME: 10 MINUTES /// COOK TIME: ABOUT 10 MINUTES

4 slices of "uncured" applewood-smoked bacon
1 tbsp olive oil
1 red onion, halved and sliced
1 tbsp ground cumin
1 tbsp ground coriander
1 tsp smoked sweet paprika
4 tbsp Banyuls or sherry vinegar
3 large, fresh cooked beetroot, peeled and cut in wedges
1 tsp unrefined granulated sugar
Kosher salt and freshly ground black pepper
60g (2oz) crumbled blue cheese
1 tbsp chopped fresh flat-leaf (Italian) parsley leaves

> Cook the bacon in a nonstick frying pan until crisp. Remove from the pan, drain on kitchen paper, and roughly break up. Set aside.

> Remove all but 1 tbsp of the bacon fat from the pan, then add the olive oil and heat. Add the onion and sauté, stirring, until lightly golden, 2–3 minutes. Add the spices and vinegar, and then the beetroot. Toss gently until they are hot, about 5 minutes. Add the sugar and season to taste.

> Spoon the beetroot onto two plates. Sprinkle the bacon on top followed by the crumbled blue cheese and then the chopped parsley. Serve with whole grain bread.

HO CHI MINH CHICKEN AND SHRIMP

SERVES 1 /// PREP TIME: 10 MINUTES /// COOK TIME: 5 ½ MINUTES

1 tbsp vegetable or sunflower oil

115g (4oz) Vietnamese vegetable mix (finely diced onion,
    green beans, and carrots)

½ tsp finely chopped lemongrass

1 small skinless, boneless chicken breast, cut in thin strips

115g (4oz) raw, peeled shrimps or small prawns, deveined if necessary

½ tsp minced garlic

3 tbsp dark soy sauce

2 tsp rice vinegar

1 tsp palm sugar or unrefined light brown sugar

½ tsp toasted sesame oil

Freshly ground black pepper

¼ head cos lettuce, shredded

> Heat the oil in a wok and stir-fry the mixed vegetables, lemongrass
and chicken for 2 minutes. Toss in the shrimp and stir-fry until they are
pink, about 1 minute longer.

> Add the remaining ingredients, except the shredded lettuce, and stir-fry
for 30 seconds.

> Pile the lettuce on a plate and spoon the chicken and shrimp mixture
on top. Serve immediately.

// To turn this into a more substantial dinner dish, add 115g (4oz) cooked
rice noodles with the soy sauce and other flavourings.

CHILLI-CORIANDER RICE

SERVES 4 /// PREP TIME: 20 MINUTES /// COOK TIME: 20 MINUTES

1 fresh habanero chilli, seeded and roughly chopped
1 fresh jalapeño chilli, seeded and roughly chopped
A large handful of fresh coriander leaves, roughly
   chopped, plus a few torn leaves for garnish
1 tsp ground cumin
Juice of 1 lemon
½ tsp kosher salt
Freshly ground black pepper
2 tbsp olive oil
450g (1lb) long grain rice
1 large white onion, chopped
2 celery sticks, chopped
2 carrots, chopped
1.2 litres (2 pints) vegetable stock
115g (4oz) raw cashew nuts (optional)
15g (½oz) butter

> Purée the chillies and chopped coriander with the cumin, lemon juice, salt, and lots of pepper in a blender, stopping occasionally to scrape down the sides as necessary.

> Heat the oil in a heavy-based pan. Add the rice and sauté, stirring, until lightly golden, about 2 minutes. Add the onion, celery, and carrots, and sauté for 1 more minute, stirring. Stir in the spice paste and then the stock. Add the cashews, if using. Bring to a boil, stirring. Reduce the heat, partially cover, and simmer gently until the rice has absorbed the liquid and is just tender, about 20 minutes.

> Stir in the butter. Taste and add more seasoning, if necessary. Serve hot or cold, garnished with torn coriander.

// When time is short, rather than making the paste, just add the minced chillies and half the coriander with the other flavourings after sautéing the vegetables. Stir in the rest of the coriander at the end of cooking.

DRAGON BREATH NOODLES

SERVES 4 /// PREP TIME: 10 MINUTES /// COOK TIME: ABOUT 5 MINUTES

1 tbsp vegetable oil
4 spring onions, finely chopped
1 tsp dried chilli flakes
2 tsp red miso paste
175ml (6fl oz) boiling water
2 garlic cloves, crushed
1 tbsp orange-blossom honey
$\frac{1}{2}$ tsp toasted sesame seeds
4 tbsp smooth peanut butter
3 tbsp tamari
1 tsp finely chopped pickled ginger
Juice of $\frac{1}{2}$ lime
450g (1lb) fresh egg noodles
Sliced red chilli or chopped red pepper for garnish

> Heat the oil in a pan. Add the spring onions and sauté for 2 minutes.
Add the remaining ingredients except the noodles. Cook, stirring, until
thickened and smooth.

> Add the noodles and toss gently until they are hot, 2–3 minutes. Garnish
with chilli or red pepper and serve, with a crisp green salad.

// These noodles are great on their own, and also work well with a piece
of grilled or barbecued fish.

ASPARAGUS AND MUSHROOM PIZZA

MAKES 4 PIZZAS /// PREP TIME: 25 MINUTES PLUS RISING /// COOK TIME: 20 MINUTES

350g (12oz) unbleached bread flour
3 tbsp wholewheat flour
25g (1oz) fine yellow cornmeal (polenta)
2 tsp kosher salt
Pinch of unrefined granulated sugar
1 sachet easy-blend dried yeast
1 tbsp olive oil
360ml (12fl oz) warm water

FOR THE TOPPING

115g (4oz) thin asparagus spears, trimmed and halved lengthways
Olive oil
450g (1lb) sliced assorted mushrooms (have fun—use shiitakes, maitakes,
    chanterelles, portobellos, and even cultivated white mushrooms)
2 large shallots or red onions, sliced
115g (4oz) shredded Savoy cabbage
115g (4oz) grated Manchego cheese
115g (4oz) grated Asiago or other melting cheese (such as Swiss)
2 tbsp chopped fresh tarragon or basil leaves
2 tbsp snipped fresh chives
2 tbsp chopped fresh flat-leaf (Italian) parsley leaves
Kosher salt and freshly ground black pepper

> First make the dough. Mix the flours with the cornmeal, salt, and sugar.
Stir in the yeast. Add the oil and then the water and mix to form a soft but
not sticky dough. Knead gently on a lightly floured surface for 5 minutes.
Place in an oiled plastic bag and let rise in a warm place until doubled in
bulk, about 1 hour.

> Alternatively, put all the ingredients in a food processor or electric mixer
fitted with the dough hook and run the machine until a ball of dough
forms. Run it for 1 minute longer, to knead the dough. Wrap and let rise.

> Knock back the dough and knead briefly until smooth. Divide into four balls. Put each ball on an oiled baking sheet and press out with your fingers to stretch evenly to a round about 20cm (8in) in diameter. Cover with oiled cling film and let rise for 30 minutes.

> Meanwhile, prepare the topping. Heat a ridged cast-iron grill pan. Brush the asparagus with olive oil and pan-grill, turning once, until bright green, slashed with brown, and just tender, about 4 minutes. Cut in short lengths on the bias and set aside.

> Heat 2 tbsp oil in the pan and sauté the mushrooms until softened, 1–2 minutes. Remove from the pan. Add another 1 tbsp oil to the pan and sauté the shallots and cabbage, stirring, until they are softening slightly, about 2 minutes.

> Preheat the oven to 220°C (425°F/Gas 7). Top the risen pizza bases with the cheeses, then the mushrooms, then the asparagus, and then the cabbage and shallot. Sprinkle with half the herbs. Drizzle with olive oil and season with a sprinkling of salt and a grinding of pepper. Bake until the crust is golden around the edges and crisp underneath, about 20 minutes. If necessary, swap the sheets halfway through cooking. Sprinkle with the remaining herbs before serving.

// For wood-barbecued pizzas, shape your dough into four pieces and let rise, then place on the hot (not too hot) side of the open kettle barbecue. Cook for about 2 minutes. Brush with olive oil and season before turning over to the other side. Add the toppings. Lower the heat (close the vents or move the pizzas to a cooler part of the barbecue), close the lid, and cook until the topping is hot throughout and the cheeses have melted, about 5 minutes.

KHMER SPRING ROLLS

MAKES 12 /// PREP TIME: 1 HOUR /// COOK TIME: 0

175g (6oz) firm tofu, drained, lightly fried in a splash
   of sunflower oil, and cut in thin strips
1 carrot, grated
3 large Chinese cabbage leaves, finely shredded
4 spring onions, finely chopped
12 fresh mint leaves, finely shredded
6 fresh Thai basil leaves, finely shredded
A handful of fresh coriander leaves, chopped
2 garlic cloves, crushed
60g (2oz) pickled ginger, chopped
1 tbsp tamari
1 tbsp palm sugar or unrefined light brown sugar
2 tbsp mixed black and white sesame seeds
A few drops of hot sauce (Sriracha or Tabasco)
Freshly ground black pepper
12 spring roll wrappers
60g (2oz) daikon sprouts

> Place everything, except the spring roll wrappers and daikon sprouts,
in a bowl. Mix well and set aside to get happy.

> Put the spring roll wrappers in a shallow dish and cover with warm
water. Let soak for 30 seconds, then drain and dry on kitchen paper. Divide
the vegetable-tofu mixture among the wrappers, leaving a 1cm (½ in)
border all around except at the top.

> Fold up the bottom of one of the skins and start rolling up from one side.
When you get three-quarters of the way, place a small amount of daikon
sprouts on top of filling, then continue rolling up completely. Roll up the
rest of the spring rolls. Arrange on a serving platter.

// For a change from daikon sprouts, use bean sprouts and lay a few
chive stems on top when rolling.

CELERIAC AND MUSHROOM SOUP

SERVES 6 /// PREP TIME: 20 MINUTES /// COOK TIME: ABOUT 30 MINUTES

1 head celeriac, about 675g (1 ¹/₂lb)
Juice of ¹/₂ lemon
25g (1oz) unsalted butter
1 small leek, white part only, finely chopped
1 shallot, finely chopped
225g (8oz) button mushrooms, thinly sliced
Leaves from 5 fresh thyme sprigs, finely chopped
4 tsp white wine vinegar
2 litres (3¹/₂ pints) chicken stock
Kosher salt and freshly ground pepper
175ml (6fl oz) double cream
Freshly grated nutmeg

> Peel the celeriac and cut into 2.5cm (1in) dice. Toss with the lemon juice and 2 tbsp water to prevent it from browning. Set aside.

> Heat the butter in a large pan. Add the leek and shallot. Sauté over low heat, stirring, until the vegetables are soft but not brown, about 3 minutes. Add the mushrooms and continue to cook gently, stirring occasionally, until they release their juices.

> Drain the celeriac and add with half the thyme. Continue to cook gently, stirring, until the pan is almost dry, taking care not to brown anything. Add the vinegar and stir until the pan is almost dry again. Add the chicken stock and some salt and pepper and bring to a boil. Reduce the heat to medium and simmer until the liquid has reduced by about half and the vegetables are really tender, about 20 minutes.

> Purée the soup in a blender until smooth, then pass through a fine-mesh sieve back into a clean pan. Stir in the cream and season to taste with nutmeg, salt, and pepper. Reheat but do not boil. Ladle into bowls and sprinkle with the remaining thyme. Serve hot.

TURKEY-AVOCADO-CARROT WRAP

MAKES 1 /// PREP TIME: 10 MINUTES /// COOK TIME: 0

1 soft flour tortilla (preferably wholewheat, but plain will do)
½ avocado, halved and stoned
A squeeze of lemon juice
1 slice Monterey Pepper Jack cheese
60g (2oz) sliced, cooked turkey breast
A small handful of baby spinach leaves
1 small carrot, grated
A little hot sauce (see Google Hot Sauce, page 249), optional

> Lay a sheet of greaseproof paper on a board and place the tortilla on top. Scoop out the avocado flesh and crush with the lemon juice, then spread across the tortilla. Top with the cheese, then the turkey, then the spinach, and last the carrot. Approach wrapping the tortilla as if it were a clock: Begin to wrap from six o'clock, continuing to wrap until the tortilla has come full circle and now resembles a cone shape.

> Peel back, reach for your favourite hot sauce—if you feel like it—and enjoy.

// If you are preparing ahead, make these in the morning—don't try to put them together the night before or the spinach will wilt and the carrot will make the tortilla damp! You can add a handful of bean sprouts to the wrap, to feel really good about your lunch, but you'll have to roll it quite tightly to hold all that filling!

ONE OR TWO OF THESE IS A GREAT LUNCH ON THE RUN.

HEIRLOOM TOMATO AND BABY LEAF SALAD

SERVES 4 /// PREP TIME: 30 MINUTES /// COOK TIME: 30 MINUTES

2 slices of rye bread, cubed
2 tbsp milk
45g (1 ½ oz) quinoa, rinsed
60g (2oz) corn kernels (fresh or thawed frozen)
60g (2oz) rocket
60g (2oz) baby spinach leaves
2 shallots, finely chopped
2 heirloom tomatoes, sliced

FOR THE VINAIGRETTE
1 tsp Dijon mustard
½ tsp ground cumin
Juice of ½ lime
3 tbsp ume plum vinegar
2 tbsp toasted sesame oil
2 tbsp sunflower oil
Kosher salt and freshly ground black pepper
2 tsp toasted sesame seeds

> Preheat the oven to 190°C (375°F/Gas 5). Toss the bread cubes in
the milk. Spread on a baking sheet and toast in the oven until crisp,
about 30 minutes. Cool.

> Cook the quinoa in boiling, lightly salted water in a small pan until just
tender, 15–20 minutes. Drain, rinse with cold water, and drain again.

> Place the corn kernels in a bowl. Add the rocket and spinach, the cooled
quinoa, and shallots. In a separate bowl, combine the mustard, cumin,
lime juice, and plum vinegar. Whisk together, then slowly whisk in the oils
until thick and smooth. Season with salt and pepper and add the toasted
sesame seeds. Drizzle the vinaigrette over the salad and toss gently.

> Arrange the sliced tomatoes on four plates. Gently pile the dressed salad
on top and garnish with the toasted rye croûtons.

APPLE AND BRIE QUESADILLAS

MAKES 8 /// PREP TIME: 20 MINUTES /// COOK TIME: ABOUT 24 MINUTES
2 Granny Smith apples
1 tbsp fresh lemon juice
About 60ml (2fl oz) olive oil
450g (1lb) rocket
Kosher salt and freshly ground black pepper
225g (8oz) just-ripe Brie cheese
8 soft whole wheat tortillas

> Peel, core, and thinly slice the apples. Toss the apple slices with the lemon juice and 2 tbsp water to prevent browning.

> Heat 1 tbsp of the olive oil in a large skillet over a moderate heat. Add a few handfuls of rocket, sprinkle lightly with salt and pepper, and move around with tongs for a few seconds until the rocket is just wilted. Transfer to a bowl. Add a little more oil to the pan and continue to wilt the remaining rocket in the same way. Set aside.

> Drain the apple slices and pat dry on kitchen paper. Divide the Brie into eight portions and spread one portion onto a tortilla. On one half of the tortilla, arrange a few slices of apple and some wilted rocket. Fold over the other half of the tortilla and press together. Repeat with the remaining tortillas, Brie, apples, and rocket.

> Heat a little olive oil in the cleaned frying pan. Put in a folded tortilla and cook over moderately high heat, pressing down with a spatula, until the base is brown and crisp. Turn over and brown the other side. Transfer the quesadilla to a chopping board. Cut into three or four wedges and keep warm. Repeat with the remaining quesadillas. Serve warm.

PEPPERED TUNA CARPACCIO

SERVES 4 /// PREP TIME: 10 MINUTES PLUS FREEZING /// COOK TIME: 0

225g (8oz) piece of fresh tuna loin
Extra virgin olive oil
2 tbsp coarsely crushed black peppercorns
Kosher or coarse sea salt
2 tbsp fresh Parmesan shavings
4 handfuls of rocket
Lemon wedges (optional)

> Brush the tuna with a little oil and roll in the peppercorns to coat completely (not the ends). Wrap tightly in cling film to form a good round shape. Place in the freezer until firm but not frozen hard, 2–3 hours.

> Unwrap the tuna and slice as thinly as possible using a sharp knife. Arrange the slices in a circle on plates. Drizzle with olive oil and sprinkle with a few grains of kosher or sea salt. Scatter a few Parmesan shavings over each portion and put a pile of rocket in the centre. If desired, serve with lemon wedges to squeeze over.

CALYPSO RICE SALAD

SERVES 4 /// PREP TIME: 15 MINUTES /// COOK TIME: 45–50 MINUTES

350g (12oz) wild rice
2 oranges
60g (2oz) redcurrants, removed from their stems
1 red pepper, diced
4 spring onions, cut in thin slices on the bias
1 small red onion, finely chopped
2 tbsp chopped fresh coriander leaves
2 tbsp chopped fresh mint leaves
1/2 tsp ground coriander
1/4 tsp cayenne
Juice of 1 small lime
3 tbsp extra virgin olive oil
1 tsp wildblossom honey
Kosher salt and freshly ground black pepper

> Cook the wild rice in a pan of boiling salted water until just tender,
45–50 minutes. Drain, rinse with cold water, and drain again well. Tip
the rice into a salad bowl.

> While the rice is cooking, peel the oranges, holding them over a
bowl to catch the juice. Be sure to cut off all the white pith. Cut the flesh
into segments, cutting down on either side of each membrane. Put the
segments to one side. Squeeze all the peel, pith, and membranes over
the bowl to collect the last of the juice, then discard. Set the juice aside.

> When the rice is ready, add the orange segments, redcurrants, red pepper,
spring and red onions, and herbs to the salad bowl.

> Add the spices, lime juice, oil, and honey to the orange juice and whisk
to mix. Season to taste. Pour this dressing over the salad and toss gently.
Serve at room temperature.

VINE-RIPE TOMATO AND BUFFALO MOZZARELLA WITH MARINATED BEETS AND ROCKET SALAD

SERVES 4 /// PREP TIME: 10 MINUTES /// COOK TIME: 0

1 large or 4 small cooked beetroot, peeled and diced

1 small shallot, finely chopped

2 tbsp red wine vinegar

4 tbsp extra virgin olive oil

1 small bunch of rocket

4 small, fresh *mozzarella di bufala* (buffalo mozzarella) balls, drained and sliced

6 small vine-ripened tomatoes, quartered

Freshly ground black pepper

> Toss the beetroot and shallot with the wine vinegar and 2 tbsp of the olive oil. Add the rocket and toss gently again. Divide among four plates.

> Arrange the mozzarella slices and tomato quarters among the rocket and beetroot. Drizzle the remaining olive oil over and season well with freshly ground pepper.

// You can use the mini-mozzarella balls called "boconccini" if you prefer bite-sized pieces of cheese.

SEATTLE JIM'S PEA SALAD

SERVES 4 /// PREP TIME: 20 MINUTES /// COOK TIME: 5 MINUTES

4 slices of "uncured" applewood-smoked bacon
225g (8oz) frozen peas, thawed
1 small red onion, diced small
115g (4oz) mangetout, cut in slices on the bias
225g (8oz) can water chestnuts, drained and sliced
2 tbsp mayonnaise
2 tbsp soured cream or crème fraîche
1 tbsp apple cider vinegar
½ tsp minced garlic
4 tbsp chopped fresh dill
Kosher salt and freshly ground black pepper

> Grill or fry the bacon until crisp. Drain on kitchen paper, then break
into small pieces.

> Dry the peas well on kitchen paper (if you don't do this, the salad will
be runny). Combine the peas, onion, mangetout, sliced water chestnuts,
and bacon in a large bowl.

> In a small bowl, whisk together the mayonnaise, soured cream or crème
fraîche, cider vinegar, garlic, and dill. Season to taste. Add to the salad
and toss gently. Serve at room temperature.

// Jim Glass was one of my sous chefs at Google. He was the kamikaze
of sous chefs. Now he's the European food director for Google. This is
a delicious salad he made up.

CAULIFLOWER-ALMOND-GARLIC SOUP

SERVES 4–6 /// PREP TIME: 30 MINUTES /// COOK TIME: 27–37 MINUTES

1 red pepper

120ml (4fl oz) olive oil

115g (4oz) flaked almonds

1 large, fresh garlic clove, peeled and very thinly sliced or chopped

½ tsp ground cumin

¼ tsp celery seed

Good pinch of cayenne

1 small cauliflower, trimmed and cut in small florets (about 350g/12oz)

225g (8oz) can of chopped tomatoes

60ml (2fl oz) cherry vinegar

1 litre (1¾ pints) good chicken stock

1 thick slice of sourdough loaf, crust removed, lightly toasted
    (centre still chewy), and cubed

Kosher salt and freshly ground black pepper

Chopped fresh parsley leaves for garnish

> Char the pepper under the grill (or hold it on the prongs of a fork over a gas flame), turning occasionally, until the skin is blackened in patches and blistering, about 15 minutes. Place in a plastic bag and let cool, then scrape off the skin with a paring knife. Cut the pepper in half, remove the stalk and seeds, and roughly chop.

> Place a heavy-based pan over low heat. Add the olive oil and almonds and let the oil heat up slowly, gently cooking the almonds until pale golden, about 10 minutes (this method of cooking the almonds is called *confit*). Add the garlic, cumin, and celery seed, and cook, stirring, for 2 minutes longer. Add the cayenne and cauliflower. Stir well, then cover and cook until the cauliflower begins to soften, about 5 minutes.

> Add the canned tomatoes, chopped pepper, and sherry vinegar, and cook, stirring, until the vinegar has almost all evaporated. Add the chicken stock. Bring to a boil, then reduce the heat and simmer until the cauliflower is soft, 20–30 minutes.

> Stir in the bread cubes, mixing well so the bread absorbs the oil and all of the toasty texture has dissolved. Purée the soup in a blender or food processor. Return to a clean pan and season to taste. Reheat before serving, garnished with chopped parsley.

ALMONDS ARE PACKED WITH VITAMIN E AND EARTHY RICH FLAVOUR. THEY CAN MOP UP DAMAGING FREE RADICALS AND KEEP YOUR BRAIN IN GREAT SHAPE.

BEETROOT SALAD WITH SHEEP'S CHEESE AND OLIVES

SERVES 4 /// PREP TIME: 10 MINUTES /// COOK TIME: ABOUT 30 MINUTES

4–5 red beetroot, about 450g (1lb) in total, trimmed,
    taking care not to cut the skin
6 tbsp extra virgin olive oil
Juice of 2 small lemons
1 small garlic clove, crushed
Kosher salt and freshly ground black pepper
4 large handfuls of rocket
175g (6oz) *ricotta salata* or feta cheese, cubed
60g (2oz) Kalamata olives, halved and pitted

> Steam the whole beetroot in a steamer, or covered metal colander over a pan of boiling water, until they are tender, about 30 minutes, depending on their size. When they are cool enough to handle, peel and cut in bite-sized chunks.

> Meanwhile, whisk together the olive oil, lemon juice, garlic, and a little salt and pepper.

> Toss the beetroot in half the dressing to coat them. Mound a generous handful of rocket on each of four plates. Arrange the beetroot, cheese, and olives over the rocket. Drizzle with the remaining dressing and add a grinding of pepper. Serve immediately.

// The tanginess from the cheese balances so well with the natural sweetness of beetroot. And the briny finish from the olives is a perfect counterpoint in this salad.

CELERIAC SALAD

SERVES 4 /// PREP TIME: 10 MINUTES PLUS CHILLING /// COOK TIME: 0

1 large head celeriac, about 675g (1 ½lb)
1 tbsp fresh lemon juice
4 tbsp mayonnaise
1 tbsp extra virgin olive oil
2 tsp Champagne vinegar
½ tsp minced garlic
1 tbsp chopped dill pickles
1 tbsp finely chopped fresh dill
1 tbsp snipped fresh chives
2 tsp finely chopped fresh thyme leaves
1 spring onion, thinly sliced
Kosher salt and freshly ground black pepper

> Peel the celeriac and coarsely shred in a food processor or cut in thin matchsticks. Place immediately in a bowl of iced water with the lemon juice added (this will prevent the celery root from browning).

> Mix together the mayonnaise, oil, vinegar, and garlic in a mixing bowl. Stir in the pickles, dill, chives, and thyme. Drain the celery root and pat dry on kitchen paper, then add to the bowl along with the spring onion. Mix gently to coat everything well. Add salt and pepper to taste. Chill until ready to serve, to let the flavours develop.

// This is good with some cubes of cheese or sliced prosciutto for a light lunch.

SUMMER VEGAN SPINACH SALAD

SERVES 4 /// PREP TIME: 25 MINUTES /// COOK TIME: 0

120g (4oz) cooked or canned chickpeas
175g (6oz) grape tomatoes, halved
25g (1oz) toasted pistachio nuts, slightly crushed
1 fresh mint sprig, torn in small pieces
250g (9oz) baby spinach leaves
60g (2oz) pea shoots
1 avocado, peeled, pitted, and diced

FOR THE DRESSING
30g (1oz) cooked or canned chickpeas
3 tbsp Dijon mustard
2 shallots, finely chopped
1 garlic clove, preferably roasted
1 tsp pickled ginger
1/4 tsp smoked paprika
1 tsp ground cumin
3 tbsp fresh orange juice
2 tbsp fresh lemon juice
2 tbsp tamari
4 tbsp sunflower oil
3 tbsp extra virgin olive oil
Kosher salt and freshly ground black pepper

> First make the dressing. Place all the ingredients, except the oils and
seasoning, in a blender and blend until fairly smooth. With the machine
running, slowly add the sunflower oil, followed by the olive oil to make
a dressing that is fairly thick and smooth. Season to taste.

> Arrange the salad ingredients in a bowl: Start with the chickpeas and
tomatoes, then the pistachios and mint, then the spinach and pea shoots,
and lastly the avocado. Trickle the dressing over, toss gently, and serve.

// If you want to take this to work for lunch, toss the avocado in lemon
juice to prevent browning, and pack the dressing separately to trickle
over the salad just before eating.

COLESLAW FOR LUNCH

SERVES 4–6 /// PREP TIME: 10 MINUTES /// COOK TIME: 0

2 tbsp pineapple juice or apple juice
4 tsp mayonnaise
2 tsp soured cream
1 tsp grated horseradish (or horseradish relish)
½ tsp white wine vinegar
Pinch of celery seed
Kosher salt and freshly ground black pepper
¼ head green cabbage, shredded
¼ small head red cabbage, shredded
2 carrots, grated

FOR SERVING
Cubes of Montery Jack cheese, crumbled crisp-cooked "uncured"
   applewood-smoked bacon, and halved cherry tomatoes

> Whisk together the pineapple juice or apple juice, mayonnaise, soured cream, horseradish, vinegar, and celery seed in a large bowl. Add salt and pepper to taste.

> Add the shredded cabbages and carrots, and toss to coat everything evenly. Store in a sealed container in the fridge until ready to use.

> To serve, top with cubes of cheese, some crumbled bacon, and halved cherry tomatoes. Eat with whole grain bread.

CHINESE TOFU SALAD

SERVES 4 /// PREP TIME: 30 MINUTES /// COOK TIME: 0

1 head cos lettuce, inner leaves only, cut across into 1cm (½in) pieces
½ small head Chinese cabbage, finely shredded
1 large red pepper, cut in thin strips
2 spring onions, cut in thin slices on the bias
200g (7oz) packet baked savoury (or smoked) tofu,
    cut into ¼in (5mm) strips
2oz (60g) fresh sunflower sprouts or bean sprouts, rinsed and drained
¼ bunch of fresh coriander leaves, coarsely chopped
2 tsp toasted sesame seeds

FOR THE WONTON CRISPS
9 wonton wrappers, thawed if frozen, cut in half and then across
    into 5mm (¼in) strips
Peanut oil for frying
Kosher salt

FOR THE DRESSING
4 tbsp grapeseed oil
1 tbsp smooth peanut butter
1 tbsp apple cider vinegar
1 tbsp rice vinegar
1 tbsp soy sauce
1 tsp dried chilli flakes
1 tbsp toasted sesame oil
2 tsp wild-blossom honey
1 garlic clove, crushed
1 tsp grated fresh root ginger
Freshly ground black pepper

> First make the wonton crisps. Heat 1cm (½in) peanut oil in a frying pan until the oil bubbles when you touch a chopstick to it (about 180°C/350°F). Add the wonton strips, a handful at a time, and fry until they are brown and crisp, about 15 seconds. Watch carefully to be sure they don't burn. As they are done, use a slotted spoon to transfer them to a plate lined with kitchen paper to drain. Sprinkle lightly with salt.

> Whisk together the grapeseed oil, peanut butter, vinegars, soy sauce, chilli flakes, sesame oil, honey, garlic, and ginger in a mixing bowl until smooth. Add salt and pepper to taste.

> Just before serving, add the lettuce, cabbage, red pepper, spring onions, tofu, sprouts, coriander, and sesame seeds to the dressing and toss to coat everything evenly.

> Pile the salad onto four serving plates and top with the wonton crisps. Serve immediately.

LOBSTER BISQUE

SERVES 4 /// PREP TIME: 25 MINUTES /// COOK TIME: 1 1/4 HOURS

15g (1/2 oz) butter
1 shallot, chopped
60g (2oz) long grain rice
1/2 tsp sweet paprika
Pinch of ground cinnamon
Juice of 1/2 lemon
A little milk
1 tbsp chopped fresh parsley

FOR THE SILKY LOBSTER STOCK
1 cooked Maine lobster
30g (1oz) butter
1 carrot, diced
1 celery stick, diced
1 turnip, diced
2 shallots, diced
1 bay leaf
120ml (4fl oz) Sauvignon Blanc or other dry white wine
1 tbsp brandy
1/4 vanilla pod
Good pinch of ground turmeric
2 fresh thyme sprigs
1 tbsp tomato purée
Kosher salt and white pepper

> First make the stock. Split the lobster in half and remove all the meat from the body and the claws. Finely chop the meat and reserve for the bisque. Melt the butter in heavy-based pan and sauté the carrot, celery, turnip, and shallots for 1 minute, stirring. Add the lobster carcass (the shells, head, and all) and the bay leaf, and sauté for 1 minute, stirring. Add the wine and boil for 1 minute. Pour the brandy into a soup ladle and ignite, then add to the pan along with the vanilla pod, turmeric, thyme, tomato purée, and 1 litre (1³/4 pints) water. Stir well. Bring to a boil. Reduce the heat to moderate, partially cover, and simmer for 1 hour. Strain the stock and season to taste.

> Rinse out the pan, and make the bisque. Melt the butter and sauté the shallot, stirring, until softened, about 1 minute. Stir in the rice and cook for 1 minute, stirring. Add the lobster stock, paprika, and cinnamon. Bring to a boil, stirring, then reduce the heat, partially cover, and simmer gently until the rice is really tender, about 10 minutes.

> Purée the mixture in a blender and pass through a sieve into a clean pan. Stir in the finely chopped lobster meat and the lemon juice. Thin with a little milk, if desired. Taste and add more seasoning, if necessary. Ladle into warm bowls and garnish with chopped parsley.

SUPER-SIMPLE AWESOME FISH TACOS

SERVES 1 /// PREP TIME: 5 MINUTES /// COOK TIME: ABOUT 6 MINUTES
3–4 frozen fish fingers (how do the square fish swim?)
1 soft flour or corn tortilla, or 2 crisp tacos
4 tsp roasted habanero salsa or other chilli salsa
30g (1oz) corn kernels (fresh or thawed frozen)
2 tbsp tartar sauce with jalapeños
A handful of shredded green or Chinese cabbage or lettuce

> Cook the fish fingers according to package directions. Warm the tortillas or shells according to package directions, too. Mix the salsa with the corn.

> Spread the tartar sauce over the tortilla or in the shells. Add the fish sticks, then the shredded cabbage or lettuce, and then the salsa-corn mix. You know what to do next. For soft tacos, roll up and eat. For crisp tacos, just munch!

// If you can't find tartar sauce with jalapeños, use ordinary tartar and add a few slices of jalapeño from a can or jar.

MIXED WHOLE GRAIN AND BERRY SALAD

SERVES 4 /// PREP TIME: 10 MINUTES /// COOK TIME: 15–20 MINUTES

115g (4oz) wheat berries
60g (2oz) kamut grains
30g (1oz) millet grains
30g (1oz) farro grains
1 head black cabbage (cavolo nero), coarsely shredded
60g (2oz) toasted flaked almonds
2 tbsp chopped crystallized ginger
4 tbsp dried blueberries or cranberries
4 tbsp extra virgin olive oil
1 tbsp white balsamic condiment
½ tsp ground cinnamon
Kosher salt and freshly ground black pepper

> Cook the wheat berries and all the grains in a pan of boiling water until just tender but still nutty, 15–20 minutes. Drain, rinse with cold water, and drain again. Tip into a large salad bowl.

> Meanwhile, bring a pan of water to a boil, add the black cabbage, and blanch for 1 minute. Drain, rinse with cold water, and drain again. Add to the grains with the almonds, ginger, and berries.

> Whisk the oil, condiment, and cinnamon together. Pour over the salad and toss gently. Season to taste and toss again. Serve at room temperature.

// This makes an amazing side dish for roasted poultry during the autumn or holidays. You can use cracked wheat instead of wheat berries, and brown rice instead of kamut.

THREE-BEAN SALAD

SERVES 4–6 /// PREP TIME: 15 MINUTES PLUS SOAKING ///
COOK TIME: 1 HOUR 10 MINUTES

115g (4oz) dried flageolet or haricot beans, soaked in cold water overnight
    (or a 400g/14oz can)
115g (4oz) dried red kidney beans, soaked in cold water overnight
    (or a 400g/14oz can)
2 fresh thyme sprigs
225g (8oz) fresh shelled or frozen broad beans
1 small onion, finely chopped
1 red pepper, finely chopped
4 Roma or plum tomatoes, seeded and diced, or 8 cherry or grape
    tomatoes, seeded and quartered
Tiny fresh mint sprigs for garnish

FOR THE VINAIGRETTE
4 tbsp extra virgin olive oil
Juice of 1 lemon
4 tbsp chopped fresh mint leaves
4 tbsp chopped fresh flat-leaf (Italian) parsley leaves
Kosher salt and freshly ground black pepper

> Drain the soaked beans and place in separate pans with the thyme.
Cover with water, bring to a boil, and boil rapidly for 10 minutes, then
reduce the heat. Cover and simmer gently until tender, about 1 hour.
Drain, rinse with cold water, and drain again. (If using canned beans,
drain and rinse them. Chop the thyme and reserve.)

> Blanch the broad beans in boiling water for 2 minutes. Drain, rinse with
cold water, and drain again.

> Mix all the beans with the onion, red pepper, and tomatoes, plus the
chopped thyme if using canned beans. Whisk the oil and lemon juice
together, and stir in the mint, parsley, and salt and pepper to taste. Pour
over the salad and toss gently. Check the seasoning, then chill to let the
flavours develop. Serve garnished with tiny sprigs of mint.

CORN AND RADISH SALAD

SERVES 4 /// PREP TIME: 15 MINUTES /// COOK TIME: 0

3 tbsp fresh lime juice
2 tbsp extra virgin olive oil
1 tbsp finely chopped jalapeño chilli (from a can or jar)
¼ tsp kosher salt
Freshly ground black pepper
1 large bunch of red radishes, stems and leaves removed
4 very fresh corn-on-the-cob
2 spring onions, cut in thin slices on the bias
A large handful of fresh coriander leaves, coarsely chopped

> Whisk together the lime juice, olive oil, jalapeño, salt, and a few grindings
of pepper in a bowl.

> Either simply slice the radishes, or cut them into 3mm (⅛in) slices,
then stack them and cut across into 3mm (⅛in) wide matchsticks.
Cut the kernels from the corn cobs.

> Add the corn, radishes, spring onions, and coriander to the dressing and
toss to coat. Add more lime juice, jalapeño, salt, or pepper to taste.

// This salad is best if covered and stored for several hours or overnight
in the fridge, to let the flavours develop.

ICED GAZPACHO

SERVES 4 /// PREP TIME: 25 MINUTES PLUS CHILLING /// COOK TIME: 6 MINUTES

2 red peppers
450g (1lb) ripe Roma or plum tomatoes
1 cucumber, peeled
1 tbsp olive oil
1 shallot, finely chopped
1 garlic clove, peeled
1 tsp ground cumin
1 tsp paprika
½ tsp ground cinnamon
2 tbsp rice vinegar
1 tsp wild-blossom honey
½ tsp grated orange zest
2 tbsp snipped fresh chives
Kosher salt and freshly ground black pepper
Fresh mint and diced vegetables for garnish

> Char and peel the peppers (see page 160). Cut in half and remove the seeds. Put the tomatoes in a bowl, cover with boiling water, leave for 30 seconds, then drain and cover with cold water. Drain again and remove the skins. Pass the tomatoes, then the cucumber, and then the pepper through the fine blade of a meat mincing attachment of an electric mixer to make a smooth purée. Alternatively, you can use a food processor.

> Heat the oil in a saucepan, add the shallot, garlic, and spices, and cook gently, stirring, until softened but not browned, about 1 minute. Add the tomato mixture along with the rice vinegar, honey, and orange zest. Bring to a boil, then reduce the heat as low as possible. Cover and simmer very gently for 5 minutes.

> Stir in the chives and season to taste. Let cool, then chill. Serve in small soup cups, each garnished with two or three ice cubes, vegetables, and mint. As the ice melts, it thins the soup to just the right consistency.

// I grind the vegetables rather than using my food processor because I like the resulting texture. Plus, it doesn't create a red foamy liquid.

SILICON VALLEY SPLIT PEA SOUP

SERVES 6 /// PREP TIME: 15 MINUTES PLUS SOAKING /// COOK TIME: 3 HOURS

1 smoked ham hock, about 1kg (2¼lb)
350g (12oz) yellow split peas, soaked in plenty of cold water
   for several hours or overnight
2 carrots, cut in small dice
2 celery sticks, cut in small dice
1 large onion, finely chopped
1 tbsp tomato purée
1 large fresh thyme sprig
1 fresh oregano sprig
1 bay leaf
1 garlic clove, crushed
1 large russet (or other floury) potato, cut in small dice
400g (14oz) can chopped tomatoes
2 tbsp chopped fresh thyme leaves
Kosher salt and freshly ground black pepper

> Put the ham hock in a pot and cover with cold water. Bring to a boil, then throw away the water (this is to make sure the finished soup isn't too salty). Put the hock back in the pot and add 2.5 litres (4½ pints) water along with the drained split peas, carrots, celery, and onion. Add the tomato purée, herb sprigs, bay leaf, and garlic. Bring to a boil. Reduce the heat to moderate, partially cover, and simmer for 2 hours.

> Lift the hock out of the pot and set aside. Discard the herb sprigs and bay leaf. Add the potato and tomatoes to the pot. Bring back to a boil and simmer, partially covered, for 1 hour longer.

> Meanwhile, when the hock is cool enough to handle, pull all the meat off the bones, discarding the fat, skin, and tendons. Dice the meat and return to the soup. Stir in the chopped thyme and season to taste.

> Serve hot, with crusty sourdough bread.

COCOA CAPONATA ON CROSTINI

SERVES 4 /// PREP TIME: 20 MINUTES /// COOK TIME: 15 MINUTES

5 tbsp olive oil
2 red peppers, diced
2 yellow peppers, diced
1 small onion, chopped
2 garlic cloves, thinly sliced
60g (2oz) pine nuts, toasted
45g (1¹/₂oz) sultanas
1 tbsp cocoa powder
60g (2oz) unrefined light brown sugar
4 tbsp red wine vinegar
4 tbsp balsamic vinegar
60g (2oz) can anchovies, drained and chopped
85g (3oz) Kalamata olives, pitted and chopped
1 tsp dried chilli flakes (or more to taste)
2 tbsp chopped fresh flat-leaf (Italian) parsley leaves
Kosher salt and freshly ground black pepper
8 slices of French bread, cut on the bias

> Heat 1 tbsp of the oil in a large pan and sauté the peppers with the onion for 3 minutes, stirring. Add the garlic, pine nuts, sultanas, cocoa powder, and sugar. Blend in the vinegars, then reduce the heat and cover. Simmer gently until most of the liquid has evaporated and the peppers are glazed and just tender, about 15 minutes. Let cool slightly, then stir in the anchovies, olives, chilli flakes, parsley, and seasoning to taste.

> Heat the remaining olive oil in a frying pan and sauté the French bread slices until golden on both sides. Drain on kitchen paper. Pile the warm caponata on the crostini and serve.

// You can rub the crostini with a cut garlic clove before topping with the caponata. It also goes great with broiled or grilled chicken or fish.

DUCK AND SHRIMP DIM SUM

MAKES 12 /// PREP TIME: 45 MINUTES /// COOK TIME: 5 MINUTES

1 small jicama or turnip, peeled and cut in chunks
1 small carrot, peeled
2 spring onions, trimmed
30g (1oz) peeled shrimps or small prawns
1 skinless duck breast, cut in pieces
60g (2oz) diced pancetta (Italian bacon)
1 tsp minced ginger
1 tsp minced garlic
1 tbsp black sesame seeds
1 tbsp black or balsamic vinegar
½ tsp toasted sesame oil
1 tbsp tamari
12 outer pak choi leaves (from 2–3 heads)
12 thin slices of fresh, hot red chilli
Sweet chilli dipping sauce for serving

> With the machine of a food processor running, drop the jicama or turnip, carrot, and spring onions into the bowl, followed by the shrimp, duck, and pancetta. When finely minced, add the remaining ingredients, except the pak choi, chilli, and dipping sauce, and pulse to mix.

> Blanch the pak choi leaves in boiling water for 45 seconds. Drain, rinse with cold water, and drain again.

> Take one leaf at a time and gently spread out on kitchen paper. Pat dry. Put a small spoonful of the filling on the green part of the leaf. Fold in the green edges, then wrap the white stem up and over, then around underneath the filling, so the package is sitting in the cup of the white stem. If necessary, gently straighten out the sides of the green so the filling is almost covered.

> Place the dim sum in a bamboo or other steamer. Cover and steam for 5 minutes.

> Serve in Asian soup spoons, with a small amount of sweet chilli dipping sauce in the bottom of each spoon and garnished with the chilli slices. Alternatively, arrange the dim sum on a platter, garnish each with a slice of chilli, and put a small bowl of dipping sauce in the centre.

// These make a great snack, but you could also serve them as an appetizer, or as a light lunch with a crisp bean sprout and shredded vegetable salad (or some rice noodles tossed in soy sauce). Use the hearts of the pak choi, shredded, in the salad.

BARLEY-CORN SALAD

SERVES 4 /// PREP TIME: 15 MINUTES /// COOK TIME: 40 MINUTES

75g (2¹/₂oz) pearl barley
Kosher salt and freshly ground black pepper
1 small red pepper
2 tbsp tamari
2 tbsp ume plum vinegar
1 tbsp soya oil
2 tsp toasted sesame oil
2 tsp finely chopped pickled ginger
2 tsp black sesame seeds
3 spring onions, cut in thin slices on the bias
1 large or 2 small corn-on-the-cob

> Bring 175ml (6fl oz) water with ¹/₄ tsp kosher salt to a boil. Add the pearl barley and cook until tender and most of the liquid has been absorbed, about 40 minutes. Leave, covered, off the heat to absorb any remaining liquid.

> Meanwhile, char the pepper under the grill (or hold it on the prongs of a fork over a gas flame), turning occasionally, until the skin is blackened in patches and blistering, about 15 minutes. Place it in a plastic bag and let cool. Scrape off the skin with a paring knife. Cut in half, remove the stem and seeds, and cut in 1cm (¹/₂in) dice.

> In a serving bowl, whisk together the tamari, vinegar, and oils. Stir in the ginger and sesame seeds. Add the spring onions and diced pepper. Toss to coat. Cut the kernels off the corn cobs and add to the bowl along with the pearl barley. Toss again. Add pepper to taste. Serve the salad warm or at room temperature.

// These are two of my favourites—cooked pearl barley and fresh corn kernels from the cob. The corn can be cooked, if you prefer, but I like the way it tastes raw in contrast to the cooked barley.

SANTA BARBARA SALAD

SERVES 1 /// PREP TIME: 15 MINUTES /// COOK TIME: 0
A large handful of baby spinach leaves, about 30g (1oz)
A large handful of rocket, about 30g (1oz)
1 small carrot, thinly sliced
4 button mushrooms, sliced
1 small beetroot, shredded
3 cherry tomatoes, halved
2 tsp toasted pumpkin seeds

FOR THE VINAIGRETTE
1/2 small shallot, finely chopped
1 tbsp extra virgin olive oil
1 tsp red wine vinegar
1/4 tsp Dijon mustard
1 tsp chopped fresh thyme leaves
1/4 tsp ground cumin
Kosher salt and freshly ground black pepper

> Whisk the vinaigrette ingredients together in a salad bowl. Add all
the salad ingredients, except the pumpkin seeds, and toss gently. Scatter
the pumpkin seeds over and serve.

DEREK, MY SURFER-COOK AT
GOOGLE, CAME UP WITH THIS.
IT HAS ALL THE GOOD THINGS
ABOUT BEING A CALIFORNIAN.

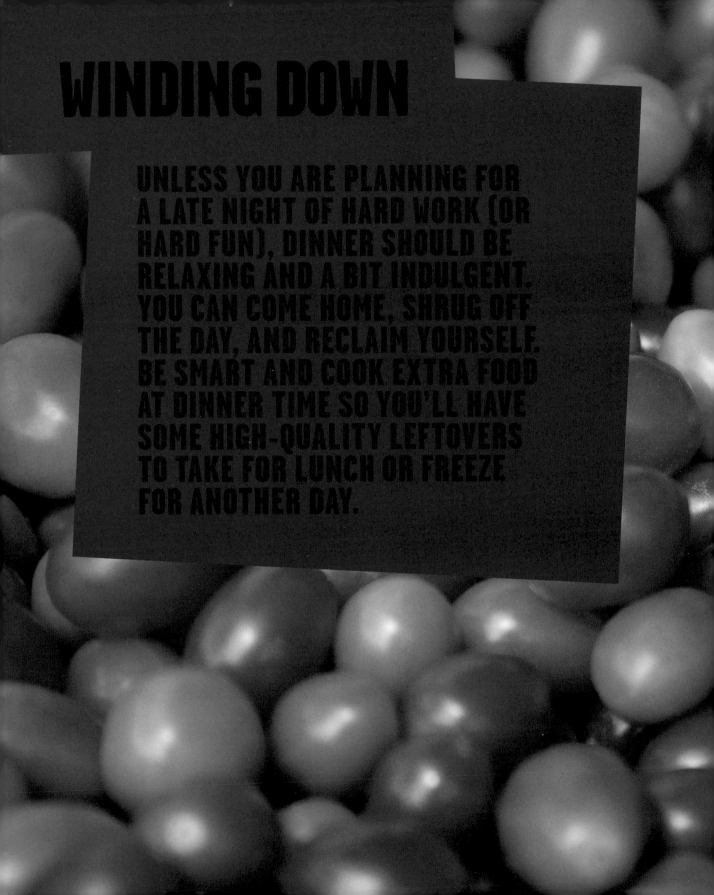

WINDING DOWN

UNLESS YOU ARE PLANNING FOR A LATE NIGHT OF HARD WORK (OR HARD FUN), DINNER SHOULD BE RELAXING AND A BIT INDULGENT. YOU CAN COME HOME, SHRUG OFF THE DAY, AND RECLAIM YOURSELF. BE SMART AND COOK EXTRA FOOD AT DINNER TIME SO YOU'LL HAVE SOME HIGH-QUALITY LEFTOVERS TO TAKE FOR LUNCH OR FREEZE FOR ANOTHER DAY.

SEARED SOUTHWESTERN AHI TUNA TORNADOES

SERVES 4 /// PREP TIME: 10 MINUTES /// COOK TIME: 3–4 MINUTES

450g (1lb) piece *ahi* (yellowfin) tuna loin (or 4 small, thick tuna steaks)
2 tbsp sunflower oil
2 tbsp Southwestern Spice Rub (see page 63)
120ml (4fl oz) mayonnaise
Juice of 1 lime
1 avocado, peeled, stoned, and mashed
1 fresh serrano chilli, seeded and finely chopped
1 shallot, finely chopped
8 soft flour tortillas
1 small jicama or turnip, grated
1 large carrot, grated
1/2 small head Chinese cabbage, shredded
A large handful of fresh coriander leaves

> Brush the tuna all over with the oil, then season with the spice rub. Heat a ridged cast-iron grill pan and sear the tuna on all sides for 3–4 minutes; the fish should still be rare in the centre. Remove from the pan and let cool, then cut in thin slices.

> Mix the mayonnaise with the lime juice, avocado, chilli, and shallot.

> Warm the tortillas. Lay each one on a piece of greaseproof paper or a napkin. Spread the mayonnaise over the tortillas, then add some jicama or turnip, then carrot, and then cabbage. Add the sliced tuna and a few coriander leaves.

> At the bottom of each tortilla, fold over one side at an extreme angle, then continue to wrap into a cone shape.

// This is a little play on sushi and southwestern foods together: I replaced the nori seaweed roll with a flour tortilla and used a spicy avocado mayonnaise instead of rice.

LAMB KORMA

SERVES 4 /// PREP TIME: 40 MINUTES PLUS MARINATING /// COOK TIME: 1 $\frac{1}{2}$–2 HOURS

2 large onions
2.5cm (1in) piece of fresh root ginger, grated
2 garlic cloves, roughly chopped
1 tsp coriander seeds, roughly crushed
1 tsp ground cumin
4 cardamom pods, split and seeds removed
½ tsp kosher salt
½ tsp dried chilli flakes
675g (1½lb) lean boneless lamb, diced
2 tbsp ghee or melted butter
2 tbsp tomato purée
120ml (4fl oz) plain yogurt
A few fresh coriander leaves, torn, for garnish

> Chop one onion; halve and slice the other. Put the chopped onion in a mortar (or small bowl) and add the ginger, garlic, coriander, cumin, cardamom seeds, salt, and chilli flakes. Pound the mixture to a paste with a pestle or the end of a rolling pin. Alternatively, use an immersion blender.

> Put the lamb in a bowl and add the spice paste. Mix well, then let marinate in a cool place or the refrigerator for at least 1 hour.

> Heat the ghee in a pan, add the sliced onion, and sauté for 2 minutes, stirring. Add the lamb and cook, stirring, until browned all over, about 5 minutes. Add the tomato purée and yogurt. Bring to a boil, stirring well, then reduce the heat, cover, and simmer gently, stirring occasionally, until the lamb is really tender and bathed in a rich sauce, 1½–2 hours.

> Spoon into a serving dish and garnish with coriander. Serve with rice, cucumber raita (thick plain yogurt mixed with fresh mint, garlic, and finely diced cucumber), and Indian relishes.

SEA BASS AND SCALLOPS WITH MINTY PEA SAUCE

SERVES 2 /// PREP TIME: 25 MINUTES /// COOK TIME: 18–20 MINUTES

1 carrot, diced

1 yellow or orange pepper, diced

1 large tomato, diced

225g (8oz) drained, canned
   cannellini beans

Kosher salt and white pepper

2 tbsp olive oil

1 Yukon Gold potato (or other all-
   purpose variety), peeled and sliced

2 small sea bass fillets, about
   115g (4oz) each, cut in half

4 king scallops

Fresh chive stalks for garnish

FOR THE MINTY PEA SAUCE

2 tsp olive oil

1 small shallot, finely chopped

½ tsp minced garlic

225g (8oz) frozen peas, thawed

2 tbsp chopped fresh mint leaves

500ml (16fl oz) chicken or
   vegetable stock

> First make the pea sauce. Heat the olive oil in a saucepan and sauté
the shallot very gently, stirring, until soft but not brown, about 1 minute.
Add the garlic, peas, mint, and half the stock. Bring to a boil, then reduce
the heat and simmer until the peas are tender, about 5 minutes. Purée
in a blender, adding enough of the remaining stock to give a thick but
pourable consistency. Return to the pan and set aside.

> While the peas are simmering, blanch the carrot in boiling water for
3 minutes; drain, rinse with cold water, and drain again. Return to the pan
and mix in the bell pepper, tomato, and beans. Season to taste. Set aside.

> Heat 1 tbsp of the olive oil in a frying pan and fry the potato slices until
golden on both sides and cooked through, about 6 minutes. Drain on
kitchen paper and keep warm. Wipe out the frying pan.

> Season the fish fillets and scallops. Heat the remaining 1 tbsp olive oil
in the frying pan until very hot but not smoking. Sauté the sea bass, skin-
side down, with the scallops until golden, 1–2 minutes. Gently turn the fish
and scallops over and quickly sear the other sides for 1–2 minutes longer.
Take care not to overcook the fish. Remove from the pan and keep warm.

> Reheat the pea sauce, and toss the bean mixture over a gentle heat to warm through. Spoon the pea sauce onto deep, warm plates, spreading it out to a large pool. Add the potato slices. Place two pieces of sea bass, skin-side down, and two scallops on top of each pool. Spoon the vegetable mixture alongside and garnish with chives.

BUTTERNUT CHILLIJACK

SERVES 4 /// PREP TIME: 20 MINUTES /// COOK TIME: 25–30 MINUTES

2 butternut squashes, peeled, seeded, and diced
2 red onions, diced
60g (2oz) sliced jalapeño chillies (from a can or jar)
1 tbsp mild chilli powder
¼ tsp cayenne (optional)
Kosher salt and freshly ground black pepper
2 tbsp grapeseed oil
2 tomatoes, diced, or 225g (8oz) drained, canned chopped tomatoes
225g (8oz) frozen corn kernels, thawed
225g (8oz) grated Monterey Jack cheese
A handful of fresh coriander leaves, torn in pieces

> Preheat the oven to 190°C (375°F/Gas 5). Combine the squash, onions, and chillies in a roasting tin and season with the chilli powder, cayenne, salt, and pepper. Drizzle the grapeseed oil over and toss well. Roast until just tender but still with some texture, 25–30 minutes.

> Remove from the oven and tip into a large bowl. Add the tomatoes, corn, Monterey jack cheese, and coriander. Mix gently until the cheese begins to melt. Serve warm.

THIS IS A SLAMMING DISH. IT WAS BORN FROM LEFTOVERS AND THE NEED TO COME UP WITH A VEGETARIAN DISH ON THE FLY AT GOOGLE.

GOAN PORK

SERVES 4 /// PREP TIME: 20 MINUTES PLUS MARINATING /// COOK TIME: 1 HOUR

4 fresh red chillies (serranos work well), seeds left in if you dare
60ml (2fl oz) rice vinegar
60ml (2fl oz) black vinegar
3 tbsp cumin seeds
2 tbsp black mustard seeds
1 tsp ground turmeric
1 tsp freshly ground black pepper
½ tsp ground cardamom
½ tsp ground cloves
Pinch of grated nutmeg (or more, depending on
    how much you like nutmeg)
1 large onion, roughly chopped
2 large garlic cloves, peeled
2.5cm (1in) piece of fresh root ginger, peeled
90ml (3fl oz) sunflower oil
1½ tbsp palm sugar or unrefined light brown sugar
1 tsp kosher salt
175ml (6fl oz) apple cider vinegar
900g (2lb) boneless pork shoulder, cut into 4cm (1½in) cubes
3 bay leaves
Fresh bay leaves for garnish

> Soak the chillies in the mixed rice and black vinegars for at least 30 minutes. Heat a small frying pan and toast the cumin and mustard seeds for 1 minute, stirring. Tip into a food processor and add the remaining spices, the onion, garlic, ginger, and chillies with their soaking vinegar. Add 1½ tbsp of the sunflower oil, the sugar, salt, and cider vinegar. Purée to a smooth paste.

> Put the diced pork in a container with a sealable lid. Stir in the curry paste, cover, and let marinate in the refrigerator overnight.

> The next day, when you are ready to cook this dish, heat the remaining oil in a heavy-based pan. Remove the pork from the marinade and braise

over a moderate heat, stirring, for 5 minutes. Add the bay leaves and the marinade, partially cover, reduce the heat and continue to cook gently, stirring occasionally, until the pork is tender and bathed in sauce, about 1 hour. During cooking, add water as needed to keep the sauce rich and thick.

> Discard the bay leaves. Taste and adjust the seasoning. Garnish with fresh bay leaves and serve with plenty of naan breads and rice.

ITALIAN CHICKEN WITH TOMATOES AND PEPPERS

SERVES 4 /// PREP TIME: 30 MINUTES /// COOK TIME: 1 HOUR

1.35kg (3lb) chicken, cut in 8 pieces
Kosher salt and freshly ground black pepper
2 tbsp olive oil
2 yellow peppers, diced
2 carrots, diced
1 large onion, finely chopped
1 large garlic clove, finely chopped
500ml (16fl oz) red wine
400g (14oz) can chopped tomatoes
60ml (2fl oz) tomato purée
2 tbsp chopped fresh oregano leaves
2 tbsp chopped fresh basil leaves

> Season the chicken. Heat the oil in a heavy-based pan. Add the chicken and brown all over. Remove from the pan. Add the peppers and carrots, and sauté until they get a little colour, about 2 minutes. Add the onion and sauté for 1 more minute. Add the garlic and wine, and boil, stirring, until reduced by half. Add the tomatoes and tomato purée. Season to taste.

> Return the chicken to the pan. Bring to a boil, then reduce the heat, cover, and simmer very gently until the chicken is really tender and the sauce is rich and thick, about 1 hour. During cooking, add a little water as necessary to prevent the sauce from becoming too concentrated.

> Add the herbs for the last 5 minutes of the cooking time. Taste and add more seasoning, if necessary. Serve with pasta or potato gnocchi.

// Toward the end of the cooking time, do not stir the chicken pieces or move them around excessively, or the meat will fall off the bones and the presentation will be spoiled.

JAPANESE BEEF CURRY

SERVES 4 /// PREP TIME: 30 MINUTES /// COOK TIME: 2 HOURS

900g (2lb) lean stewing steak, such as chuck, cut into 4cm (1½in) cubes
3 tbsp tamari
3 tbsp black or balsamic vinegar
4 tbsp rice or sunflower oil
3 tbsp plain flour
2 shallots, chopped
1 leek, white part only, sliced
1 garlic clove, thinly sliced
1cm (½in) piece of fresh root ginger, grated
1 carrot, sliced
1 small celeriac, diced
½ tsp ground turmeric
1 tsp coarsely ground black pepper
½ tbsp paprika
Good pinch of ground cloves
1 tsp ground coriander
120ml (4fl oz) spring water
1 tbsp red miso paste
2 spring onions, chopped
1 tbsp toasted sesame seeds

> Toss the beef in 1 tbsp each of the tamari and vinegar. Heat 3 tbsp of the oil in a large, heavy-based pan. Sprinkle in the flour and cook until slightly browned, about 1 minute. Add the beef and sauté, stirring, until browned, about 5 minutes. Remove the beef from pan.

> Add the remaining 1 tbsp oil and heat it, then sauté the shallots, leek, garlic, and ginger for 2 minutes. Add the carrot, celeriac, and spices, and cook for 30 seconds, stirring. Add the remaining 2 tbsp vinegar.

> When the vinegar has almost all evaporated, return the beef to the pan. Stir well, then add the spring water and miso. Bring to a boil. Reduce the heat, partially cover, and simmer very gently until the meat and vegetables are very tender, about 2 hours. Season with the remaining tamari. Serve spooned over rice, garnished with the spring onions and sesame seeds.

LAMB BURGERS WITH TZATZIKI SAUCE

SERVES 4 /// PREP TIME: 15 MINUTES PLUS CHILLING /// COOK TIME: 6–8 MINUTES

450g (1lb) good-quality lamb mince
1 tsp minced garlic
½ tsp ground cloves
1 tsp ground cumin
Kosher salt and freshly ground black pepper
1 tbsp olive oil
4 artisan-style hard rolls
4 small handfuls of baby spinach leaves

FOR THE MARINATED ONIONS
½ red onion, thinly sliced
1 tbsp red wine vinegar
1 tsp unrefined light brown sugar

FOR THE SAUCE
5cm (2in) piece of cucumber, coarsely grated
60ml (2fl oz) Greek-style plain yogurt
¼ tsp minced garlic
2 tbsp chopped fresh mint leaves

> Put the lamb in a bowl and add the garlic, cloves, cumin, and plenty of freshly ground black pepper. Mix with your hands until well combined, then shape into four burgers. Chill until ready to cook.

> Mix the red onion with the vinegar and sugar. Let marinate while you prepare the sauce. Squeeze the cucumber to remove excess moisture, then mix with the yogurt, garlic, mint, and a little salt and pepper. Chill.

> When ready to eat, heat a ridged cast-iron grill pan. Sprinkle the burgers with a little kosher salt and brush with olive oil. Cook the burgers until browned and cooked through, 3–4 minutes on each side.

> Meanwhile, split the rolls and toast them. When the burgers are cooked, assemble your creation with baby spinach leaves, tzatziki sauce, and the drained marinated onions.

GRILLED SALMON-PESTO-TOMATO BUNDLES

SERVES 2 /// PREP TIME: 25 MINUTES /// COOK TIME: 25 MINUTES

10 thin asparagus spears
225g (8oz) cooked long grain rice
2 pieces of wild salmon fillet, about 115g (4oz) each
Kosher salt and freshly ground black pepper
2 tbsp olive oil
2 vine-ripened tomatoes, halved
2 tbsp fresh breadcrumbs
2 tbsp pesto (from a jar or refrigerated tub)
2 lemon wedges

> Blanch the asparagus in boiling water for 2 minutes. Drain, rinse with cold water, and drain again. Preheat the grill.

> Lay two sheets of foil on the grill rack and top each with a piece of baking parchment. Put half of the rice in the centre of each piece of parchment. Lay five asparagus spears on each mound of rice and top with a salmon fillet. Season with salt and pepper, and drizzle with the olive oil. Place the tomatoes on the fish. Mix the breadcrumbs and pesto together and spoon this over the tomatoes.

> Place under the grill, about 12.5cm (5in) from the heat, and cook for 5 minutes. Remove from the heat. Turn off the grill and switch the oven on to 190°C (375°F/Gas 5).

> Carefully pull up all four sides of each sheet of foil over the filling and gently tuck the edges together to create a teepee-shaped bundle. Make sure the edges of each bundle are sealed tightly. Return to the oven and cook for 20 minutes longer.

> Place the bundles on plates, open up the foil, and serve with wedges of lemon to squeeze over.

LINGUINE WITH PORTUGUESE CLAM SAUCE

SERVES 4 /// PREP TIME: 15 MINUTES /// COOK TIME: 22 MINUTES

450g (1lb) fresh clams, scrubbed and any open ones discarded
  (or a 300g/10oz can clams)
1 tsp dried chilli flakes
500ml (16fl oz) V8 vegetable juice
Juice of ½ lemon
1 tsp dried oregano
1 garlic clove, crushed
350g (12oz) linguine
15g (½oz) butter
Kosher salt and freshly ground black pepper

> If using fresh clams, put them in a large pan with about 1cm (½in) boiling water. Cover and steam for 5 minutes, shaking the pan occasionally. Drain, reserving 250ml (8fl oz) of the cooking liquor. Discard any clams that have not opened. (If using canned clams, drain them and reserve the juice.)

> Put the chilli flakes in a pan and toast gently, stirring, until fragrant, about 1 minute. Take care not to burn them. Add the vegetable juice and clam cooking liquor (or juice from the can). Bring to a boil and boil rapidly until reduced by half, about 10 minutes. Add the lemon juice and oregano, and simmer for 5 minutes longer. Stir in the garlic.

> While the sauce is simmering, cook the linguine according to package directions. Drain the pasta and return to its pot. Stir in the clam sauce and butter. Add the clams. Toss gently over low heat for 1 minute. Taste for salt – it should taste like the ocean – and then serve.

// You could use Clamato juice instead of V8. With canned clams, the prep time will be only 5 minutes.

MEXICAN CHICKEN AND CAPER STEW

SERVES 4–6 /// PREP TIME: 25 MINUTES /// COOK TIME: 40 MINUTES

1 red pepper
8 skinless, boneless chicken thighs, diced
250ml (8fl oz) chicken stock
4 potatoes, diced
1 onion, roughly chopped
2 tomatoes, chopped
2 tbsp capers, roughly chopped
500ml (16fl oz) pineapple juice
4 tbsp dry white wine
1 bay leaf
1 tsp ground cumin
3/4 tsp dried oregano
Kosher salt and freshly ground black pepper
2 tbsp roughly chopped fresh coriander leaves

> Char the pepper under the grill (or hold it on the prongs of a fork over a
gas flame), turning occasionally, until the skin is blackened in patches and
blistering, about 15 minutes. Place in a plastic bag and let cool, then scrape
off the skin with a paring knife. Cut the pepper in half, remove the stalk
and seeds, and cut in dice.

> Place the chicken in a heavy-based pan with the chicken stock. Bring
to a boil, then reduce the heat and simmer for 10 minutes. Add the diced
pepper and all the remaining ingredients, except the coriander, and bring
back to a boil. Reduce the heat again and simmer until the chicken and
potatoes are tender, about 30 minutes.

> Taste and add more seasoning, if necessary. Discard the bay leaf, garnish
with the coriander, and serve with plain rice.

// This is also good with 2 tbsp sliced jalapeños (from a can or jar) added
with the capers.

FILET MIGNON WITH MELTED CURLY ENDIVE

SERVES 2 /// PREP TIME: 30 MINUTES /// COOK TIME: 25 MINUTES

6–8 small fingerling potatoes, scrubbed
2 baby carrots, scrubbed
5 tbsp olive oil
Kosher salt and freshly ground black pepper
2 filet mignon steaks, about 115g (4oz) each, trimmed
1 small head curly endive, halved (or 2 wedges of a larger head)
2 shallots, finely chopped
1 tsp minced garlic
1 cup frozen peas, thawed
4 tsp Banyuls or sherry vinegar
3 tbsp white miso broth
15g (1/2oz) unsalted butter
1 tbsp chopped fresh basil leaves

> Preheat the grill. Place the potatoes and carrots on a large sheet of foil. Drizzle with 2 tbsp of the olive oil, season with salt and pepper, and add 2 tbsp water. Bring the corners of the foil together and fold over to form a sealed parcel. Place on the grill rack and cook under the grill, about 12.5cm (5in) from the heat, for 25 minutes.

> Brush the steaks with a little oil. When the potato parcel has been cooking for 15 minutes, add the steaks to the grill rack and cook to your liking (2–6 minutes on each side). Remove from the grill and keep hot. Place the curly endive on the grill rack and broil until it wilts and is lightly caramelized on the outside, 3–5 minutes.

> Meanwhile, heat the remaining oil in a frying pan, add the shallots, and sauté, stirring, until just turning golden, about 2 minutes. Add the garlic and peas, and stir well. Add the vinegar and bubble until it has almost all evaporated, then stir in the miso broth, butter, and basil.

> Open the foil parcel. Place three or four potatoes in the centre of each plate, set a steak on the potatoes, and top with the melted curly endive. Spoon the pea mixture over and around, and rest a carrot gently next to each steak with its tip pointing up. Serve immediately.

ORANGE FIRE CHICKEN

SERVES 4 /// PREP TIME: 7 MINUTES /// COOK TIME: 2 HOURS

4–6 skinless, boneless chicken breasts, cut in chunks
1/4 tsp habanero chilli powder
Finely grated zest of 1/2 orange
3 tbsp tomato passata
1 tbsp tomato purée
1/4 tsp ground cinnamon
2 tsp shredded pickled ginger
1 tsp ground coriander
1/4 tsp sweet smoked paprika
500ml (16fl oz) Sauvignon Blanc or other dry white wine
1 bay leaf
2 tsp toasted sesame seeds
1 1/2 tbsp unrefined light brown sugar
1 tsp minced garlic
4 tbsp tamari
Kosher salt and freshly ground black pepper
1 tbsp chopped fresh parsley leaves

> Put all the ingredients, except the parsley, in an enamelled cast-iron pot and stir well. Bring to a boil. Reduce the heat to as low as possible, cover, and simmer very gently for 1 3/4 hours.

> Remove the lid of the pot, turn up the heat slightly, and simmer, stirring occasionally, until the sauce has reduced and thickened, about 15 minutes. Taste and add more seasoning, if necessary. Serve over couscous, quinoa, or rice, garnished with chopped parsley.

// Cast iron is a solid conductor of heat and retains its own heat really well, so you need to cook over a very low temperature.

SNAPPER IN A YOGURT COAT

SERVES 4 /// PREP TIME: 30 MINUTES PLUS SOAKING AND MARINATING ///
COOK TIME: 20 MINUTES

1 whole red snapper (or striped
　bass or white bass), about
　1.35kg (3lb), cleaned and scaled,
　fins removed
Freshly ground black pepper
Chopped fresh flat-leaf (Italian)
　parsley
Fresh lemon juice
4 ripe tomatoes, sliced

FOR THE YOGURT COAT
45g (1½oz) raisins
3 tbsp boiling water
500ml (16fl oz) thick, plain yogurt
1½ tsp ground cumin
1 tsp ground turmeric
1 tsp ground ginger
½ tsp ground cinnamon
1 tsp white pepper
3 tbsp fresh lemon juice
½ tsp minced garlic
1 tsp fish sauce
1 tbsp white sesame seeds

> First make the yogurt coat. Soak the raisins in the boiling water until
plumped and soft, about 30 minutes. Place in a food processor, add the
rest of the coat ingredients, and blend until smooth.

> Make a few slanted cuts along the sides of the fish, about 1in (2.5cm)
long. Cover the fish in the yogurt coat and refrigerate for 2–4 hours.

> Preheat the grill. Place the fish in a foil-lined grill pan. Spoon enough of
the yogurt marinade over to cover the fish and grind some pepper over it.
Broil, about 12.5cm (5in) from the heat, for 10 minutes. The coating on the
fish will go from a yellowish brown to golden brown, and then to dark
brown very fast. Watch carefully to be sure it doesn't burn.

> Turn the fish over, coat with more of the yogurt marinade, and grind
more pepper over. Grill for 10 minutes longer. To make sure it doesn't
get too brown, turn off the grill just as the colour is turning brown.

> Let the fish rest for a few moments, then set it on a bed of chopped
parsley on a platter. Squeeze some lemon juice over the fish and layer
sliced tomatoes on top. Serve with couscous and steamed greens.

SEITAN OR QUORN WELLINGTONS

SERVES 4 /// PREP TIME: 20 MINUTES PLUS COOLING /// COOK TIME: 15–20 MINUTES

30g (1oz) unsalted butter
2 shallots, finely chopped
225g (8oz) button mushrooms, thinly sliced
2 tbsp chopped fresh thyme
250ml (8fl oz) good drinking red wine
½ tsp minced garlic
Kosher salt and freshly ground black pepper
4 large sheets filo pastry
1 tbsp sunflower oil
8 bite-sized pieces of seitan or 4 Quorn cutlets
Fresh parsley sprigs for garnish

> Melt the butter in a frying pan and sauté the shallots, stirring, until softened, about 1 minute. Add the mushrooms and stir until they begin to soften. Add the thyme, wine, garlic, and a little salt and pepper. Simmer, stirring, until the wine has almost evaporated but the mixture is still moist. Let cool.

> Preheat the oven to 190°C (375°F/Gas 5). Brush the sheets of filo with a little oil and fold in half to form squares. Brush lightly with oil again. Spoon the mushroom mixture onto the centre of the squares. Top with either two pieces of seitan or a Quorn cutlet. Season with salt and pepper. Fold the pastry over the filling to form sealed parcels. Place sealed-side down on a lightly oiled baking sheet. Brush the parcels with a little oil.

> Bake until crisp and golden, 15–20 minutes. Cut the wellingtons in half and arrange on serving plates. Garnish with sprigs of parsley and serve with creamed potatoes and a crisp green salad.

ORANGE-MARINATED CHICKEN WITH CARROT-HARISSA PASTA

SERVES 4 /// PREP TIME: 20 MINUTES PLUS MARINATING ///
COOK TIME: ABOUT 20 MINUTES

4 skinless, boneless chicken breasts
Finely grated zest and juice of 1 orange
2 tsp wild-blossom honey
1 tbsp olive oil
1 tsp minced garlic
Kosher salt and freshly ground black pepper
350g (12oz) fusilli pasta

FOR THE SAUCE
1 tsp caraway seeds
½ tsp cumin seeds
1 tsp dried chilli flakes
1 tbsp pickled ginger, squeezed dry and finely chopped
1 tsp minced garlic
500ml (16fl oz) carrot juice (preferably freshly made)
Finely grated zest of 1 orange
400g (14oz) can chickpeas, drained
15g (½oz) butter
4 handfuls of baby spinach leaves

> Make several slashes in each chicken breast, so the marinade flavours
will soak in. Lay the chicken in a shallow dish in a single layer. Whisk the
orange zest and juice with the honey, oil, garlic, and a little salt and pepper.
Pour this over the chicken. Turn to coat completely, then let marinate in
a cool place or the refrigerator for at least 1 hour.

> Toast the caraway and cumin seeds with the chilli flakes in a pan until
they become fragrant, about 2 minutes. Crush in a clean coffee grinder or
mortar and pestle (or in a bowl with the end of a rolling pin). Return to the
pan and add the ginger, garlic, carrot juice, and orange zest. Bring to a boil.
Reduce the heat and simmer gently until reduced by half, about 10 minutes.

> Add the chickpeas and butter, and simmer for 5 minutes longer. Throw the spinach into the pan, cover, and cook until wilted, about 2 minutes. Season to taste.

> While the sauce is simmering, cook the pasta according to package directions; drain and return to the pot. At the same time, heat a ridged cast-iron grill pan, drain the chicken (reserve the marinade), and pan-grill until lightly browned and cooked through, 3–4 minutes on each side.

> Add the chickpea sauce to the pasta and toss well. Pour any remaining marinade and 2–3 tbsp water into the grill pan and bubble for a few seconds, stirring well.

> Pile the pasta on warm plates and put a piece of chicken alongside the pasta. Spoon the juices over and serve.

// For the pasta sauce, you can cheat and use 2 tbsp ready-made harissa paste mixed with the carrot juice and orange zest, instead of blending the toasted spices, garlic, and ginger.

DO I REALLY HAVE TO REMIND YOU THAT SPINACH IS GOOD FOR YOU? IT TASTES SO GOOD YOU WOULD EAT IT ANYWAY.

FILET MIGNON WITH CRISP BACON, SEARED POLENTA, AND WILTED SPINACH SALAD

SERVES 4 /// PREP TIME: 20 MINUTES /// COOK TIME: 12 MINUTES

4 filet mignon steaks, about 115g (4oz) each, trimmed
2 tbsp tamari
Freshly ground black pepper
8 slices of "uncured" applewood-smoked bacon,
    each cut in thirds
1 red onion, finely chopped
1 garlic clove, thinly sliced
4 golden tomatoes, halved
4 vine-ripened tomatoes, halved
3 tbsp Muscat or Chardonnay wine vinegar
2 tbsp chopped fresh thyme leaves
Finely grated zest of 1 lemon
250g (9oz) baby spinach leaves
500g (18oz) packet ready-made plain polenta,
    cut in 8 slices
A little olive oil
2 tbsp chopped fresh flat-leaf (Italian) parsley leaves

> Season the steaks with the tamari and ground pepper, and let marinate while you prepare the rest of the dish. Preheat the grill.

> Fry the bacon in a wok until crisp, about 5 minutes. Remove from the wok, drain on kitchen paper, and keep warm.

> Add the onion and garlic to the bacon fat and sauté, stirring, until softened and just turning lightly golden, about 2 minutes. Add the tomatoes and cook until softening but still holding their shape, about 3 minutes. Add the vinegar and bubble for a few seconds until almost evaporated. Add the thyme, lemon zest, and spinach. Season to taste. Stir gently until the spinach wilts, about 2 minutes. Remove from the heat.

> While the vegetable mixture is cooking, brush the polenta slices and steaks with a little olive oil and place them on the grill rack about

12.5cm (5in) from the heat. Grill the polenta slices until they are golden brown, about 3–4 minutes on each side. Grill the steaks to the desired degree of doneness (2–6 minutes on each side).

> Reheat the wilted spinach. Transfer the steaks and polenta to warm plates and spoon the bacon, wilted spinach, and tomatoes alongside. Sprinkle with the parsley and serve.

BALSAMIC-FIG PORK CHOPS WITH BLUE CHEESE MASHED POTATOES

SERVES 4 /// PREP TIME: 25 MINUTES /// COOK TIME: 15–20 MINUTES

4 fresh rosemary sprigs

4 boneless pork chops, about
175g (6oz) each

4 slices of "uncured" smoked bacon

1 tsp Southwestern Spice Rub
(see page 63)

A little vegetable oil

4 tbsp balsamic-fig vinegar (or
ordinary aged balsamic)

A few fresh rosemary sprigs
for garnish

FOR THE POTATOES

675g (1 1/2lb) Yukon Gold (or other
all-purpose potatoes), peeled and
quartered lengthwise

2 tbsp crumbled blue cheese

2 tbsp soured cream or crème fraîche

15g (1/2oz) butter

1 tbsp milk

2 tbsp snipped fresh chives

Kosher salt and freshly ground
black pepper

> Place a sprig of rosemary in the centre of each chop, then wrap a bacon slice around it. Season with the spice rub. Keep chilled until needed.

> Heat a ridged cast-iron grill pan. When hot, brush it with oil and add the pork chops, rosemary-side down. Cook for 10 minutes, turning the heat down to moderate after the first 2 minutes. Turn the chops over and cook for another 10 minutes. Drizzle the balsamic vinegar over the chops. Turn the heat down to low and finish cooking, 5–10 minutes longer.

> While the chops are cooking, boil the potatoes in lightly salted water until tender, 15–20 minutes. Drain, reserving the cooking water, and return to the pan. Use a potato masher to mash the potatoes with the cheese, cream, butter, and milk. Add the snipped chives and beat with a wooden spoon or electric mixer just until smooth and fluffy. Season to taste.

> When the chops are cooked, transfer to plates and keep warm. Pour enough potato cooking water into the grill pan to cover the bottom. Bring to a boil, scraping up any meat residues. Taste the *jus* you've made and season, if necessary. Spoon the *jus* over the pork chops and spoon the potatoes alongside. Garnish with rosemary sprigs and serve.

LOBSTER SALAD WITH VANILLA VINAIGRETTE

SERVES 2 /// PREP TIME: 1 HOUR /// COOK TIME: 0

1 avocado

Fresh lemon juice

1–2 fresh palm hearts, peeled and
  sliced (or use canned)

1 tbsp extra virgin olive oil

1 good-sized cooked Maine lobster

4 moist, semi-dried tomatoes

½ tsp minced garlic

1 tsp chopped fresh thyme leaves

1 mango, peeled, stoned, and
  finely diced

2 small handfuls of baby salad leaves

FOR THE VANILLA VINAIGRETTE

Juice of 1 orange, strained

¼ vanilla pod

1 tsp wild-blossom honey

2 tbsp extra virgin olive oil

2 tbsp vegetable oil

Fresh lemon juice, strained

Kosher salt and white pepper

> First make the dressing. Put the orange juice in a small bowl. Split the vanilla pod and scrape the seeds into the bowl (discard the pod). Add the honey, then gradually whisk in the olive oil followed by the vegetable oil. Add lemon juice, salt, and pepper to taste.

> Peel, stone, and finely dice the avocado. Toss with a squeeze of lemon juice, to prevent browning. Season the palm hearts with 1 tsp lemon juice, a little salt and pepper, and the olive oil.

> Split the lobster in half. Remove the black vein that runs down the length of the body and lift out the tail meat. Cut in neat dice. Carefully remove the meat in one piece from each large claw.

> Stand a 5cm (2in) tall cylinder mould that is 6cm (2½in) wide on a large serving plate. Arrange half the palm heart slices in the mould. Top with 2 tomatoes, pressing down slightly with a spoon. Lightly smear with garlic and sprinkle with thyme. Gently top with about one-third of the diced avocado, then one-third of the mango, and then add half the diced lobster tail, arranged attractively. Press down very gently with your fingers. Carefully lift off the mould. Repeat with a second plate.

> Whisk the vinaigrette again to combine, then spoon about 1 tbsp over each tower. Garnish the plates with the remaining diced avocado and mango. Gently place a shelled lobster claw against each tower. Lightly drizzle additional vinaigrette around the plates and garnish the towers with a few baby salad leaves.

// You can use 4 artichoke hearts (cooked or canned) instead of palm hearts, and prawns instead of lobster, garnishing with large prawns.

STEAMED DUO OF SOLE AND HALIBUT WITH RAINBOW PEPPER STIR-FRY

SERVES 2 /// PREP TIME: 40 MINUTES /// COOK TIME: 7 MINUTES

2 small sole fillets (or 1 large sole or flounder fillet, halved lengthwise)

2 pinches of ground cumin

115g (4oz) piece of boneless halibut (or any meaty white fish), cut in half

2 fresh mint leaves

2 fresh chive stalks

2 tsp rice vinegar

2 tsp tamari

1 tsp black sesame seeds

A few fresh chive stalks for garnish

FOR THE STIR-FRY

2 tbsp sunflower or vegetable oil

4 spring onions, cut in short lengths on the bias

1 red pepper, cut in thin strips

1 yellow pepper, cut in thin strips

115g (4oz) pea shoots

1 fresh, hot, red chilli, such as a Thai chilli, seeded and chopped

350g (12oz) fresh egg noodles or cooked soba noodles

1 tsp cumin seeds

1 tsp caraway seeds

1cm (1/2in) piece of fresh root ginger, grated

1 garlic clove, very thinly sliced

2 tbsp tamari

> Lay the sole fillets, membrane-side up, on a board. Season each fillet with a pinch of cumin, then place a halibut portion in the centre. Lay the mint on the halibut, then wrap the sole fillet around the halibut. Tie up each parcel with a chive stalk (be gentle so the chive doesn't break).

> Place the parcels in a bamboo steaming basket, or other steamer, lined with baking parchment. Season the fish with the rice vinegar and tamari, and sprinkle with the sesame seeds. Steam for 7 minutes.

> Meanwhile, heat the oil in a wok and stir-fry the onions, peppers, pea shoots, and chilli for 3 minutes. Add the noodles, spices, ginger, garlic, and tamari, and stir-fry for 2 minutes longer.

> Spoon the stir-fry onto plates and arrange the fish alongside. Garnish with a few chive stalks and serve.

TOFU WITH SPINACH AND CHILLIES

SERVES 4 /// PREP TIME: 5 MINUTES /// COOK TIME: ABOUT 10 MINUTES

2 tbsp ghee or melted butter
1 small onion, chopped
1 tsp minced garlic
1½ tsp minced fresh root ginger
1 tsp ground turmeric
½ tsp cumin seeds
1 tsp black mustard seeds
360ml (12fl oz) tomato passata
1–2 fresh jalapeño chillies, seeded and finely chopped
450g (1lb) firm tofu, drained and diced
4 handfuls of baby spinach leaves
Freshly ground black pepper
1 lime, cut in wedges

> Heat the ghee or butter in a pan and sauté the onion with the garlic and ginger, stirring, until softened and fragrant, about 2 minutes. Add the turmeric, cumin seeds, and mustard seeds. When the mustard seeds begin to pop, add the passata and chillies, and gently stir in the tofu. Bring to a boil. Reduce the heat and simmer very gently for 5 minutes.

> Add the spinach, cover, and cook gently until slightly wilted, 2–3 minutes longer. Season with pepper. Spoon into bowls, squeeze lime juice over, and serve with brown rice.

TORTELLONI WITH CREAMY BROAD BEANS AND THYME

SERVES 3–4 /// PREP TIME: 10 MINUTES /// COOK TIME: 8 MINUTES

175g (6oz) shelled fresh or thawed frozen broad beans
300ml (10fl oz) strong chicken stock
3 tbsp cooked long grain rice
60g (2oz) freshly grated Parmesan, plus extra for serving
1 large garlic clove, thinly sliced
2 tbsp chopped fresh thyme leaves
Freshly grated nutmeg
Kosher salt and freshly ground black pepper
350g (12oz) fresh tortelloni stuffed with cheese and ham
2 tbsp crème fraîche or double cream
10g (¹/₄oz) butter

> Blanch the broad beans in boiling water for 3 minutes. Drain and rinse with cold water, then slip the beans out of their skins.

> Put the stock, two-thirds of the broad beans, and the rice in a pan. Bring to a boil and boil for 5 minutes, stirring occasionally. Purée in a blender with the cheese, garlic, and thyme until smooth. Return to the pan. Season to taste with nutmeg, salt, and pepper.

> Cook the tortelloni according to packet directions. Drain.

> Add the cream, butter, and remaining beans to the puréed bean sauce and heat through. Add the tortelloni and toss gently to coat. Serve with extra grated Parmesan.

// If you don't have any cooked rice, use a small potato, peeled and grated. After puréeing, this pasta sauce can be frozen in ice cube trays, for later use. Add the finishing touches when you thaw and reheat it.

SPANISH RICE

SERVES 4 /// PREP TIME: 5 MINUTES /// COOK TIME: 20 MINUTES

2 tbsp grapeseed oil
1 onion, chopped
1 garlic clove, crushed
1½ tsp mild chilli powder
1 tsp ground cumin
1½ tsp chopped jalapeño chillies (from a can or jar)
350g (12oz) long grain rice
250ml (8fl oz) dry white wine
400g (14oz) can chopped tomatoes
500ml (16fl oz) boiling chicken stock
Kosher salt and freshly ground black pepper
2 tbsp chopped fresh thyme leaves

> Heat the oil in a pan and sauté the onion gently, stirring, until softened but not browned, about 2 minutes. Add the garlic, spices, and chillies, and cook, stirring, for 1 minute longer.

> Stir in the rice until it is glistening, then add the white wine. Boil rapidly until the wine has been absorbed. Add the tomatoes and simmer until the tomato juices are almost all gone, about 2 minutes.

> Stir in the stock. Bring back to a boil, then reduce the heat, cover, and simmer gently until the liquid is absorbed and the rice is tender, about 15 minutes. Season to taste, and stir in half the thyme. Garnish with the remaining thyme and serve hot.

// Serve this with pan-grilled large prawns, salmon, tuna, or chicken.

WILD SALMON AND WARM BEET SALAD

SERVES 4 /// PREP TIME: 15 MINUTES /// COOK TIME: 30 MINUTES

1 bunch of red beetroot, greens and stems on
5 tbsp olive oil
2 yellow peppers, cut in chunks
4 slices "uncured" applewood-smoked bacon, diced
1 bunch of spring onions, sliced
2–4 garlic cloves, thinly sliced
Kosher salt and freshly ground black pepper
4 thick pieces of wild salmon fillet, about 140g (5oz) each
A few grains of *fleur de sel* (French sea salt)
Juice of 2 oranges
About 4 tsp aged balsamic vinegar

> Remove the greens and stems from the beetroot, wash well, chop, and reserve. Peel the beetroot and cut in chunks. Heat 2 tbsp of the oil in a large, heavy-based frying pan. Add the beetroot to one side of the pan, the peppers to the other. Cover and pan-roast over a moderate heat, turning once or twice, until tender, about 30 minutes.

> Meanwhile, heat 2 tbsp of the remaining oil in a wok. Add the bacon and sauté until golden, about 2 minutes. Add the spring onions and garlic, and sauté for 1 minute longer. Add the chopped beetroot stems and greens. Stir-fry until wilted but still with some "bite," about 5 minutes. Season to taste. Remove from the wok with a draining spoon and set aside.

> Season the salmon fillets with *fleur de sel* and pepper. Heat the remaining oil in the wok. Sear the salmon, skin-side down, until crisp and golden, about 3 minutes. Turn the fillets over, add the orange juice, and cook for 3 minutes longer.

> Add the wilted greens to the cooked beetroot and peppers, and toss gently to heat through. Transfer to warm plates. Place the salmon fillets on top and spoon any pan juices over. Drizzle aged balsamic vinegar over each portion and serve.

FARFALLE WITH TUNA, WILTED SPINACH, SUN-DRIED TOMATOES, AND PINE NUTS

SERVES 4 /// PREP TIME: 5 MINUTES /// COOK TIME: 14–16 MINUTES

350g (12oz) farfalle (bowtie) pasta
2 tbsp olive oil
1 garlic clove, crushed
2 tsp harissa paste
350g (12oz) tuna loin, cubed
350g (12oz) baby spinach leaves
4 sun-dried tomatoes in olive oil, drained and chopped
12 cherry tomatoes, halved
120ml (4fl oz) chicken stock
60g (2oz) sliced black olives
Kosher salt and freshly ground black pepper
Juice of 1/2 lemon
60g (2oz) toasted pine nuts

> Cook the pasta in plenty of boiling salted water for about 10 minutes, or according to packet directions. Drain and toss with 1 tbsp of the olive oil.

> While the pasta is cooking, heat the remaining olive oil in a large frying pan. Add the garlic and harissa, and stir for a moment until they are fragrant. Add the tuna and sauté for 1–2 minutes. Add the spinach and move it around with tongs until it begins to wilt. Stir in the sun-dried tomatoes, cherry tomatoes, chicken stock, and olives. Bring to a boil and simmer until the cherry tomatoes have softened but are still holding their shape, about 2 minutes. Season with salt and pepper and sharpen with lemon juice.

> Stir in the pasta and toss well. Pile into warm, shallow pasta bowls and garnish with the pine nuts.

FATTOUSH

SERVES 4 /// PREP TIME: 25 MINUTES /// COOK TIME: 0

2 Roma or plum tomatoes, seeded and diced

2 spring onions, thinly sliced

1 yellow pepper, diced

1 cucumber, peeled and diced

1/4 small red onion, chopped

A handful of fresh mint leaves, roughly chopped

A handful of fresh flat-leaf (Italian) parsley leaves, coarsely chopped

125g (4 1/2oz) trimmed watercress or rocket

115g (4oz) cubed feta cheese

85g (3oz) stoned Kalamata olives

FOR THE PITTA TOASTS

2 pitta breads, split in half lengthwise

2 tsp extra virgin olive oil

1 1/2 tsp *za'atar* (or 1/2 tsp each dried thyme, ground sumac, and sesame seeds, mixed together)

FOR THE DRESSING

4 tbsp extra virgin olive oil

2 tbsp fresh lemon juice

1 small garlic clove, crushed

Kosher salt and freshly ground black pepper

> Preheat the oven to 180°C (350°F/Gas 4). Brush one side of the pitta bread halves with olive oil and sprinkle with 1 tsp of the *za'atar*. Toast in the oven until the pittas are crisp and pale golden, 10–12 minutes. Set aside to cool.

> Whisk the dressing ingredients together in a large mixing bowl. Season to taste. Add the tomatoes, spring onions, pepper, cucumber, red onion, mint, parsley, watercress or rocket, cheese, and olives to the bowl. Toss to coat everything evenly.

> Break the pittas into rough bite-size pieces and add them to the salad. Sprinkle with the remaining *za'atar*, and toss again. Taste and season with more salt, pepper, and lemon juice, if necessary. Serve immediately.

SEITAN OR QUORN CABBAGE SUSHI

MAKES 36 PIECES /// PREP TIME: 45 MINUTES /// COOK TIME: 25 MINUTES

6 large Savoy cabbage leaves

1 small aubergine

60g (2oz) drained seitan or
Quorn, minced

200ml (7fl oz) coconut milk

2 tbsp chopped fresh basil leaves

2 tsp Thai green curry paste

30g (1oz) rice noodles

4 shiitake mushrooms, sliced

Juice of ½ lime

1½ tsp rice vinegar

2 tsp palm sugar or unrefined
light brown sugar

1 small bunch of fresh mint

1 small carrot, grated

A handful of pea shoots

2 tsp black onion or sesame seeds

Tamari for serving

> Blanch the cabbage leaves in about 2.5cm (1in) boiling water for
3 minutes. Drain, reserving the water. Rinse the leaves with cold water,
then pat dry with kitchen paper. Remove the large rib toward the
bottom of each leaf. Refrigerate the leaves until needed.

> Cook the whole aubergine in the cabbage water, covered, until tender
when a knife is inserted through it, 15–20 minutes. Drain, rinse with cold
water, and let cool.

> Simmer the seitan or Quorn in the coconut milk, stirring frequently,
until thickened, about 5 minutes. Remove from the heat and stir in the
basil and curry paste. Peel the aubergine, chop, and stir into the seitan or
quorn mixture. Spread out on a plate to cool, then chill.

> Cook the noodles for a minute or so longer than recommended on the
packet, so they are slightly sticky. Drain and let cool, then chill.

> Mix the mushrooms with the lime juice, rice vinegar, and sugar. Chill.

> When ready to assemble, lay a sheet of cling film on a clean work surface.
Cover with a bamboo rolling mat and lay another sheet of cling film on this.
Put a cabbage leaf on top, gently easing the two points together where the
rib was cut out. Lay two or three mint leaves on the cabbage and then one-
sixth of the sticky noodles. Spread one-sixth of the aubergine mixture over

the noodles, then add some of the carrot, then marinated mushrooms, and then a few pea shoots. Using the bamboo mat, roll up tightly, taking care not to roll the cling film inside the cabbage roll. Wrap the roll in the cling film and chill. Repeat with the remaining ingredients to make six long rolls in all.

> When ready to serve, trim the ends off the rolls and cut each one into six pieces. Arrange the sushi on plates. Sprinkle each piece with a few black onion or sesame seeds and a few drops of tamari.

// This also makes a stylish light lunch. If you don't have a rolling mat, use a sheet of heavy-duty foil.

TOFU NIÇOISE

SERVES 4 /// PREP TIME: 25 MINUTES /// COOK TIME: 0

3 tbsp extra virgin olive oil
Juice of 1/2 lemon
1/2 tsp Dijon mustard
1 garlic clove, crushed
1 small courgette, sliced
1/2 small red onion, thinly sliced
115g (4oz) thin green beans, trimmed, steamed until tender, and drained
115g (4oz) sun-dried tomatoes in oil, drained and halved
60g (2oz) stoned Niçoise olives
2 tsp pickled capers
4 fresh flat-leaf (Italian) parsley sprigs, chopped
450g (1lb) firm tofu, drained and cubed
Kosher salt and freshly ground black pepper

> Whisk together the olive oil, lemon juice, mustard, and garlic in a medium bowl. Add the courgette, red onion, beans, tomatoes, olives, capers, and half the parsley, tossing to coat everything well.

> Add the tofu and toss gently, being careful not to break it up. Season with salt and pepper to taste. Serve garnished with the remaining parsley.

THAI FORBIDDEN RICE SALAD

SERVES 4 /// PREP TIME: 10 MINUTES /// COOK TIME: 30 MINUTES

225g (8oz) Thai black rice (also called forbidden rice)
Kosher salt and freshly ground black pepper
2 tbsp tamari
2 tsp toasted sesame oil
Juice of ½ lime
½ tsp *sambal oelek* or hot chilli paste
115g (4oz) roasted, unsalted cashews
½ red pepper, finely chopped
½ yellow pepper, finely chopped
6 spring onions, thinly sliced

> Put the rice, 500ml (16fl oz) water, and a pinch of salt in a pan. Bring to a boil, then cover, reduce the heat, and simmer gently until the liquid is absorbed and the rice is tender, about 30 minutes.

> Meanwhile, whisk the tamari, sesame oil, lime juice, and *sambal oelek* or chilli paste together in a salad bowl. Add the cashews, red and yellow peppers, and spring onions.

> When the rice is ready, add it to the mixture and toss to coat everything well. Add salt, pepper, and additional *sambal oelek* or lime juice to taste. Serve warm or at room temperature.

// If you can't get Thai black rice, try wild rice, or wild rice mixed with long grain rice, instead, and cook according to packet directions.

PICK ME UP

IN THE WORKING DAY, YOU NEED REGULAR PITSTOPS TO UP YOUR FUEL INTAKE. SNACKS AND GRAB-AND-GO WRAPS SHOULD BE SIMPLE, MESS-FREE COMBINATIONS THAT BUILD UP AN EXCITING FLAVOUR PROFILE WITH CONTRASTING TEXTURES AND TASTES. AVOID MESSY, DRIPPY FOOD AND YOU WON'T BE WIPING IT OFF YOUR KEYBOARD OR YOUR DESK.

BANANA-PEANUT BUTTER WRAP—GREEN TEA

SERVES 1 /// PREP TIME: 5 MINUTES /// COOK TIME: 0

1 soft wholewheat or corn tortilla
2 tbsp smooth peanut butter
2 tbsp orange-blossom honey
1 banana
A squeeze of lemon juice
1 cup of strong-brewed green tea

> Lay the tortilla on a sheet of greaseproof paper. Spread with the peanut butter and then the honey. Thinly slice the banana and toss with the lemon juice to prevent browning (particularly if you aren't going to eat this right away). Fold the tortilla in half and half again to make a triangular cone, then fill with the sliced banana. Enjoy with a cup of green tea.

TAKE THIS ONE TO WORK.

GRAB & GO

DRIED MANGO—JERKY—SUNFLOWER SEEDS

SERVES UP TO 4 /// PREP TIME: 2 MINUTES /// COOK TIME: 0

175g (6oz) packet all-natural beef jerky
115g (4oz) dried mango
225g (8oz) unsalted toasted sunflower seeds

> Eat the above ingredients together for a quick mid-morning snack.

// You can exchange ingredients to fit your lifestyle – try dried cranberries and pumpkin seeds with turkey jerky for a change.

GRAB & GO

SUNFLOWER SEEDS ARE AN EXCELLENT SOURCE OF "HAPPY-MAKING" B VITAMINS.

APPLE—YOGURT—ALMONDS

SERVES 1 /// PREP TIME: 3 MINUTES /// COOK TIME: 0

1 apple, sliced
250ml (8fl oz) vanilla yogurt
175g (6oz) toasted almonds

> Just simply eat until full. Save what you haven't finished for later.

GORGONZOLA AND WALNUT CROSTINI

SERVES 1 /// PREP TIME: 2 MINUTES /// COOK TIME: 6–7 MINUTES

1–2 thick slices of wholewheat walnut bread
2–4 tsp wild-blossom honey
30–60g (1–2oz) creamy Gorgonzola cheese
A few edible flowers

> Preheat the grill. Lightly toast the bread on both sides under
the grill. Spread the toast with the honey and then with the cheese.
Grill until the cheese melts and is just turning golden around the
edges, 2–3 minutes. Garnish with a few edible flowers and eat.

DRIED CHERRY CHUTNEY WITH GOAT'S CHEESE AND CRACKERS

MAKES 1 JAR /// PREP TIME: 5 MINUTES /// COOK TIME: 10 MINUTES

175g (6oz) dried cherries
85g (3oz) unrefined light brown sugar
90ml (3fl oz) sherry vinegar
2 tbsp finely chopped crystallized ginger
4 tbsp apple juice
2 tbsp fresh lemon juice
½ tsp dried chilli flakes
Pinch of ground cardamom

FOR SERVING
Goat's cheese, wholegrain crackers, and tender young celery sticks

> Put all the ingredients in a small, heavy-based pan. Bring to a boil, then reduce the heat and simmer over a moderate heat until thickened, about 10 minutes. Pot, cool, and label. It will keep in the fridge for several weeks.

> To serve, slice cylinders of goat's cheese, using a wet knife, and arrange on plates with some wholegrain crackers and celery. Add a heaped spoonful of the chutney to each plate.

// This chutney is also great with cold meats and curries.

SMOKED SALMON—SUN-DRIED CRANBERRIES—GOAT'S CHEESE WRAP

SERVES 1 /// PREP TIME: 6 MINUTES /// COOK TIME: 0

1 soft wholewheat tortilla
About 30g (1oz) goat's cheese
2 slices of smoked wild salmon
1 tbsp sun-dried cranberries
A handful of beansprouts or daikon sprouts

> Lay a sheet of greaseproof paper on a board. Put the tortilla on top. Spread the goat's cheese across the tortilla, followed by the smoked salmon. Strew the sun-dried cranberries over and, finally, top with the sprouts.

> Looking at the tortilla as if it were a clock, begin to roll from six o'clock and continue all the way around to make a cone. Secure in the paper.

GOOD SNACKS KEEP YOU FROM EATING JUNK, AND HELP PREVENT YOU FROM OVEREATING AT THE NEXT MEALTIME.

SPINACH LATKES

MAKES 12 /// PREP TIME: 15 MINUTES /// COOK TIME: 6–8 MINUTES

3 potatoes (preferably russet), about 450g (1lb) in total, peeled
60g (2oz) chopped fresh wilted spinach (or thawed frozen spinach)
1 small onion, grated
3 tbsp matzo meal or unbleached plain flour
Kosher salt and freshly ground black pepper
2 eggs, beaten
Vegetable or grapeseed oil

> Grate the potatoes into a bowl. Squeeze the potatoes to drain off excess moisture. Squeeze out the moisture from the spinach. Drain the onion. Mix all the vegetables together and stir in the matzo meal or flour, some seasoning, and the eggs.

> Pour enough oil into a frying pan to coat the bottom and heat over a moderate heat. Put three spoonfuls of the mixture in the pan, spaced well apart, and press out to make cakes about 10cm (4in) diameter. Cook until golden brown, about 3–4 minutes on each side. Keep the latkes warm in a low oven while cooking the remainder.

> Serve with a fresh herb salad dressed with vinaigrette.

I CAME UP WITH THESE FOR HANUKKAH, WHICH WAS THE FIRST HOLIDAY WE EVER CELEBRATED AT GOOGLE.

WATERMELON SATÉ WITH HONEY-VINEGAR DIPPING SAUCE

SERVES UP TO 8 /// PREP TIME: 10 MINUTES /// COOK TIME: 2 MINUTES

6 tbsp orange-blossom honey
4 tbsp sherry vinegar
¼ tsp ground cinnamon
¼ tsp habanero chilli powder
¼ tsp kosher salt
1 small watermelon

> First prepare the sauce. Put the honey, vinegar, cinnamon, chilli powder, salt, and 1 tbsp water in a small saucepan and bring to a boil, stirring. Remove from the heat and pour into a small dish. Let cool, then chill.

> Cut wedges from the melon (as much as you like). Peel them and remove the seeds, if desired, then cut in chunks. Thread the chunks onto small wooden skewers.

> When you are ready to serve this amazingly refreshing snack, just platter up as many of the melon skewers as you need, place the dipping sauce on the platter, and go out and make some people happy.

// You get the five S's with this dish: sweet, sour, salty, spicy, and slightly savoury – not exactly umami! If you're not sharing with friends, you probably won't eat a whole watermelon at once, but make all the dipping sauce. Store it in the fridge and then you can make more saté sticks whenever you fancy a snack.

SWEET POTATO SCONES

MAKES ABOUT 15 /// PREP TIME: 30 MINUTES /// COOK TIME: 15 MINUTES

1 small sweet potato, cut in small chunks
225g (8oz) unbleached plain flour
1 tbsp baking powder
½ tsp bicarbonate of soda
½ tsp ground cinnamon
½ tsp fine sea salt
60g (2oz) cold unsalted butter, cut in 6 pieces
250ml (8fl oz) buttermilk
2 tbsp wild-blossom honey

> Cook the sweet potato in boiling water until soft, about 6 minutes.
Drain and mash well.

> Preheat the oven to 220°C (425°F/Gas 7). Line a baking sheet with a
silicone baking mat or baking parchment.

> Sift the flour, baking powder, bicarbonate of soda, cinnamon, and salt
into a bowl. Cut the butter into the flour mixture with two knives or a
pastry blender (or use your cool fingertips to rub it in) until the mixture
resembles coarse crumbs.

> In a separate bowl, mix the buttermilk, mashed sweet potato, and honey.
Mix the potato mixture into the flour mixture until just combined.

> Turn the mixture onto a floured board and knead gently, one or two
times, just to bring the dough together. Press out into a round about
1cm (½in) thick. Cut out biscuits using a 7.5cm (3in) round cutter or glass.
Knead the trimmings and cut out more scones.

> Arrange a little apart on the baking sheet. Bake until the scones are
golden, about 15 minutes. Remove to a rack to cool slightly. Serve warm,
split open, with butter and honey.

SMOKED SALMON TARTLETS

MAKES 12 /// PREP TIME: 20 MINUTES /// COOK TIME: 8–10 MINUTES

6 large, rectangular sheets of filo pastry
1–2 tbsp sunflower oil
200g (7oz) Neufchâtel or cream cheese
1 tbsp milk
2 tbsp snipped fresh chives
2 tsp fresh lemon juice
115g (4oz) smoked wild salmon trimmings or slices, chopped
Kosher salt and freshly ground black pepper
60g (2oz) jar of salmon caviar

> Preheat the oven to 190°C (375°F/Gas 5). Brush a sheet of filo pastry with a little oil and fold in half. Brush with a little oil again. Cut in half to form two oblongs. Fold these in half to form squares. Brush with oil again. Repeat with the remaining sheets of filo. Press the squares into 12 lightly oiled individual tartlet tins. Bake until crisp and golden, 8–10 minutes. Let cool.

> Beat the cheese with the milk, chives, and lemon juice. Separate the pieces of salmon and mix in. Season the mixture to taste.

> When ready to serve, spoon the salmon mixture into the filo cases and garnish each with a small spoonful of salmon caviar.

MINT-CHOCOLATE BROWNIES

MAKES 16 /// PREP TIME: 30 MINUTES /// COOK TIME: ABOUT 35 MINUTES

175g (6oz) unsalted butter
175g (6oz) bitter chocolate
175g (6oz) unbleached plain flour
2 tbsp cocoa powder
1/2 tsp fine sea salt
4 eggs
450g (1lb) unrefined granulated sugar
1 tsp peppermint extract
1 tsp pure vanilla extract
2 cups bittersweet or plain chocolate chips

> Preheat the oven to 180°C (350°F/Gas 4). Butter a 20cm (8in) square
baking tin and set aside.

> Melt the butter and chocolate together in a double boiler or in a bowl
set over, but not touching, simmering water in a pan. Stir until smooth.
Remove from the heat and let cool.

> Sift the flour, cocoa powder, and salt into a small bowl. Beat the eggs
and sugar together with an electric mixer until very thick and pale,
and the beaters leave a trail when lifted out of the mixture. Mix in the
melted chocolate and the peppermint and vanilla extracts at lowest
speed. Fold in the flour mixture and the chocolate chips, mixing just
until the batter is no longer streaky.

> Transfer the batter to the prepared pan. Bake until a skewer inserted about
2.5cm (1in) from the edge comes out clean, about 35 minutes. The top should
feel set, but the centre should still be quite soft. (If the skewer comes out very
wet, test another place to be sure you didn't poke into a melted chocolate chip.)
Transfer the tin to a rack to cool and cut into squares when cold. Store the
brownies in an airtight container.

COCONUT-OATMEAL BARS WITH CHOCOLATE CHIPS

MAKES 16 /// PREP TIME: 15 MINUTES /// COOK TIME: 25 MINUTES

60g (2oz) unbleached plain flour
¼ tsp baking powder
¼ tsp fine sea salt
115g (4oz) rolled oats
115g (4oz) unrefined light brown sugar, lightly packed
60g (2oz) dried, unsweetened, dessicated coconut
60g (2oz) bittersweet or semisweet chocolate chips
85g (3oz) unsalted butter, melted and cooled to room temperature
1 large egg, lightly beaten
¼ tsp natural vanilla extract

> Preheat the oven to 180°C (350°F/Gas 4). Lightly oil an 8in (20cm) square baking tin and set aside.

> Sift the flour, baking powder, and salt into a mixing bowl. Stir in the oats, brown sugar, coconut, and chocolate chips. Stir together the melted butter, egg, and vanilla, then add to the flour mixture and stir just until blended. Avoid mixing more than needed. Transfer to the prepared pan and level the surface.

> Bake until slightly risen, golden, and just firm to the touch, about 25 minutes. Put the tin on a rack and let cool before cutting into triangular or rectangular bars or squares.

PACK THESE IN YOUR BAG AND EAT THEM ON THE WAY TO WORK.

GOOGLE HOT SAUCE

MAKES 1 JAR /// PREP TIME: 15 MINUTES /// COOK TIME: 45 MINUTES

115g (4oz) fresh habanero chillies, roughly chopped
45g (1½oz) fresh jalapeño chillies, roughly chopped
1 dried chipotle chilli, crushed
2 tbsp tomato purée
1 tbsp minced ginger
1 tbsp tamarind paste
1 tbsp pomegranate molasses
1 ½ tbsp apple cider vinegar
90ml (3fl oz) fresh orange juice
4 tsp unrefined light brown sugar
Juice of 1 lime
1 small carrot, finely diced
1 small onion, finely chopped
1 celery stick, finely chopped
2 tbsp Worcestershire sauce
1 tbsp Thai fish sauce
3 tbsp good drinking red wine

> Place all the ingredients in a heavy-based pan. Add 120ml (4fl oz) water.
Bring to a boil, then reduce the heat, cover, and simmer very gently, stirring
occasionally, until rich and thick and the vegetables are very soft, about
45 minutes.

> Purée in a blender, then pass through a sieve. Add a little more
water to thin to the desired consistency. Store in a clean, sealed jar in
the fridge. Serve to fire up any of the recipes that call for chilli sauce,
or use on tacos, crostini, wraps, or even peanut butter sandwiches!

INDEX

///: A

apple and brie quesadillas 153
apple cider vinegar 44, 45
apple-oaty thing, quick 132
apple–yogurt–almonds 234
apricot multigrain breakfast 126
asparagus and mushroom pizza 144

///: B

bacon: beetroot with bacon and crumbled blue cheese 138
filet mignon with crisp bacon, seared polenta, and wilted spinach salad 210
balsamic-fig pork chops with blue cheese mashed potatoes 213
balsamic vinegar 45
banana-peanut butter wrap–green tea 232
Banyuls vinegar 45
barley 50
barley-corn salad 184
beans 52–53
to freeze 67
three-bean salad 174
tortelloni with creamy fava beans and thyme 218
beef: dried mango–jerky–sunflower seeds 233
filet mignon with crisp bacon, seared polenta, and wilted spinach salad 210
filet mignon with melted frisée 203
Japanese beef curry 197

beer 97
beetroot: beet-carrot-ginger fizz 34
beetroot salad with sheep's cheese and chives 163
beetroot with bacon and crumbled blue cheese 138
vine-ripe tomato and buffalo mozzarella with marinated beets and rocket salad 157
wild salmon and warm beetroot salad 221
berries: black and blue yogurt fru fru 108
cranberry-orange bread 135
fruity sesame-seed granola 129
Hawaiian kitchen-sink smoothie 111
mixed wholegrain and berry salad 173
peaceful berry morning smoothie 117
smoked salmon–sun-dried cranberries–goat's cheese wrap 235
smoothie sandia 117
Washington nutty-blue smoothie 120
black and blue yogurt fru fru 108
bread 96
cranberry-orange bread 135
breakfast tacos 131
broiled salmon-pesto-tomato bundles 200
brown rice vinegar 45
brownies, mint-chocolate 245
butternut chillijack 193

///: C

calypso rice salad 156
caponata on crostini, cocoa 180
caramelized mushroom sauce 71
carbohydrates (carbs) 54
carrot-celery-apple juice 34
carrot-cucumber lemonade 34
carrot-ginger-orange juice 34
carrot-parsley juice 35
carrots for snacking 75
cauliflower-almond-garlic soup 160
celery root and mushroom soup 150
celery root salad 164
cheese 81
apple and brie quesadillas 153
beetroot salad with sheep's cheese and olives 163
beetroot with bacon and crumbled blue cheese 138
butternut chillijack 193
cheese grits 50
dried cherry chutney with goat's cheese and crackers 235
fattoush 224
gorgonzola and walnut crostini 234
smoked salmon–sun-dried cranberries–goat's cheese wrap 236
vine-ripe tomato and buffalo mozzarella with marinated beets and rocket salad 157
cheese-flavoured oils 49
chicken: Ho Chi Minh chicken

and shrimp 141
hot chicken wings 61
Italian chicken with
    tomatoes and peppers 196
Mexican chicken and caper
    stew 202
orange fire chicken 204
orange-marinated chicken
    with carrot-harissa
    paste 208
chilli-cilantro rice 142
chilli-infused vinegar 61
chilli sauces 58–61, 255
    Google hot sauce 249
Chinese black vinegar 44, 45
Chinese tofu salad 168
chocolate 97
    coconut-oatmeal squares
        with chocolate chips 246
    mint-chocolate brownies
        245
chutney-yogurt crust 90
cider vinegar, apple 44, 45
citrus crusher 110
citrus oils 48
coating, Japanese mayo 90
cocoa caponata on crostini 180
coconut-oatmeal bars with
    chocolate chips 246
coleslaw for lunch 167
condiments 88–90
cool and spicy tomato soup 71
corn meal 50
corn and radish salad 175
cranberry-orange bread 135
creamy breakfast polenta 130
crostini, cocoa caponata on 180
    gorgonzola and walnut 234
crush, three-melon 35
crusty miso glaze 90
curry, Japanese beef 197
curry pastes 91

III: D
dim sum, duck and shrimp 182
dragon breath noodles 143

dreamy peach smoothie 108
dried cherry chutney with
    goat cheese and crackers
    235
dried mango–jerky–sunflower
    seeds 233
duck and shrimp dim sum 182

III: E
eggs 18, 77
equipment 100

III: F
farfalle with tuna, wilted
    spinach, sun-dried
    tomatoes, and pine
    nuts 223
farro 50, 255
fast food 12, 30
fattoush 224
fennel pollen 255
fermented foods 38
filet mignon with crisp bacon,
    seared polenta, and
    wilted spinach salad 210
filet mignon with melted
    frisée 203
fish 82–83
    broiled salmon-pesto-
        tomato bundles 200
    farfalle with tuna, wilted
        spinach, sun-dried
        tomatoes, and pine
        nuts 223
    to freeze 72–73
    peppered tuna carpaccio
        155
    raw 36–37
    sea bass and scallops with
        minty pea sauce 190
    seared Southwestern ahi
        tuna tornadoes 188
    smoked salmon–sun-dried
        cranberries–goat's
        cheese wrap 236
    smoked salmon tartlets 244

snapper in a yogurt
    coat 206
steamed duo of sole and
    halibut with rainbow
    pepper stir-fry 216
super-simple awesome
    fish tacos 171
wild salmon and warm
    beetroot salad 221
fish sauce 91, 255
flavour cubes 68–69
flax seed 51
fluffy soy pancakes 124
fondue, mystery 81
food labels 18
freezer storage times 65
freezing 64
fruit: to freeze 66
    fresh 28
fruit salad salsa 29
fruity sesame-seed granola
    129

III: G
garlic, to slice 100
garlicky chilli-chicken
    cubes 69
gazpacho, iced 176
glace de vien 92
glaze, crusty miso 90
Goan pork 194
Google hot sauce 249
gorgonzola and walnut
    crostini 234
granola 127
    fruity sesame-seed 129
grains 50
    apricot multigrain
        breakfast 126
    to freeze 67
    mixed wholegrain and
        berry salad 173
great salad to keep in the
    fridge 30
greens, raw 75
grits, cheese 50

III: H

halibut: steamed duo of sole and halibut with rainbow pepper stir-fry 216
Hawaiian kitchen-sink smoothie 111
heirloom tomato and baby leaf salad 152
herb salt 93
herbs, homegrown 98, 99
Ho Chi Minh chicken and shrimp 141
hot chicken wings 61

III: I

iced gazpacho 176
Indian chutneys 88
Italian chicken with tomatoes and peppers 196

III: J

jade smoothie 113
Japanese beef curry 197
Japanese mayo coating 90
Japanese mayonnaise 88, 89, 255
Japanese ume plum vinegar 44, 45
juice, carrot-celery-apple 34
carrot-ginger-orange 34
carrot-parsley 35
pineapple-grapefruit 35

III: K

kamut 50, 255
ketchup 88, 89
ketchup glaze 90
ketchup, roasted jalapeño 90
Kewpie mayonnaise 255
Khmer spring rolls 148
kimchi, Nina's 38

III: L

lamb burgers with tzatziki sauce 199
lamb korma 189

latkes, spinach 239
lemon-shallot vinaigrette 46
lemonade, carrot-cucumber 34
linguine with Portuguese clam sauce 201
lobster bisque 170
lobster salad with vanilla vinaigrette 214
locally grown food 14, 22

III: M

malt vinegar 45
Manchego oil 49
mandolin slicer 100
mayonnaise 89
Japanese 88, 89, 255
meat: to freeze 72–73
"uncured" deli meats 86
see also beef; lamb; pork
mellow miso broth cubes 69
Mexican chicken and caper stew 202
microwave ovens 101
milk 76
millet 50
mint-chocolate brownies 245
miso broth cubes, mellow 69
miso paste 88
mixed wholegrain and berry salad 173
Moroccan carrot-harissa cubes 69
Mount Shasta fruit smoothie 121
mushrooms: asparagus and mushroom pizza 144
caramelized mushroom sauce 71
celery root and mushroom soup 150
mystery fondue 81

III: N

Nina's kimchi 38

noodles, dragon breath 143
nuts 51
gorgonzola and walnut crostini 234

III: O

oils 48
olive oil 48
orange carrot cabaret 118
orange fire chicken 204
orange-marinated chicken with carrot-harissa paste 208
orange-miso vinaigrette 46
organic food 12, 14, 17

III: P

pancakes, fluffy soy 124
Parmesan oil 49
pasta: to cook 54
farfalle with tuna, wilted spinach, sun-dried tomatoes, and pine nuts 223
linguine with Portuguese clam sauce 201
tortelloni with creamy fava beans and thyme 218
peaceful berry morning smoothie 117
peach smoothie, dreamy 108
peppered tuna carpaccio 155
pineapple-grapefruit juice 35
pizza, asparagus and mushroom 144
plum vinegar, ume 44, 45
polenta: creamy breakfast polenta 130
filet mignon with crisp bacon, seared polenta, and wilted spinach salad 210
pork: balsamic-fig pork chops with blue cheese mashed potatoes 213
Goan pork 194

///: Q

quesadillas, apple and brie 153
quick apple-oaty thing 132
quinoa 50
Quorn cabbage sushi 226
Quorn wellingtons 207

///: R

raw food 12, 26, 30
raw juice drinks 34–35
recycling 101
rice 54
    calypso rice salad 156
    chilli-cilantro rice 142
    to cook 55
    Spanish rice 220
    Thai forbidden rice
        salad 229
rice-bran oil 48
rice vinegar 44, 45
roasted jalapeño ketchup 90

///: S

salad drawer 74–75
salads: barley-corn salad 184
    beet salad with sheep's
        cheese and olives 163
    calypso rice salad 156
    celery root salad 164
    Chinese tofu salad 168
    coleslaw for lunch 167
    corn and radish salad 175
    fattoush 224
    great salad to keep in the
        fridge 30
    heirloom tomato and baby
        leaf salad 152
    lobster salad with vanilla
        vinaigrette 214
    mixed wholegrain and
        berry salad 173
    Santa Barbara salad 185
    Seattle Jim's pea salad 158
    summer vegan spinach
        salad 166
    Thai forbidden rice

salad 229
    three-bean salad 174
    tofu niçoise 227
    vine-ripe tomato and
        buffalo mozzarella with
        marinated beets and
        rocket salad 157
    wild salmon and warm beet
        salad 221
salmon: broiled salmon-pesto-
        tomato bundles 200
    smoked salmon–sun-dried
        cranberries–goat cheese
        wrap 236
    smoked salmon tartlets 244
    wild salmon and warm
        beetroot salad 221
salsa, fruit salad 29
salts 47
Santa Barbara salad 185
sauces: caramelized
        mushroom sauce 71
    to freeze 70
    Google hot sauce 249
scones, sweet potato 243
screwy rabbit... think
        brunch! 114
sea bass and scallops with
        minty pea sauce 190
seafood 82, 83
    duck and shrimp dim
        sum 182
    Ho Chi Minh chicken and
        shrimp 141
    linguine with Portuguese
        clam sauce 201
    lobster bisque 170
    lobster salad with vanilla
        vinaigrette 214
    sea bass and scallops with
        minty pea sauce 190
    seared Southwestern ahi tuna
        tornadoes 188
Seattle Jim's pea salad 158
seeds 51
    dried mango–jerky–

sunflower seeds 233
    fruity sesame-seed granola
        129
    granola 127
seitan cabbage sushi 226
seitan wellingtons 207
sherry vinegar 45
Silicon Valley split pea
        soup 179
slow cooker 100
smoked salmon–sun-dried
        cranberries–goat's cheese
        wrap 236
smoked salmon tartlets 244
smoothies: citrus crusher 110
    dreamy peach smoothie 108
    Hawaiian kitchen-sink
        smoothie 111
    jade smoothie 113
    Mount Shasta fruit
        smoothie 121
    orange carrot cabaret 118
    peaceful berry morning
        smoothie 117
    smoothie sandia 117
    smoothoccino 123
    wake-up breakfast
        smoothie 121
    wake-up shake-me-up
        power shake 118
    Washington nutty-blue
        smoothie 121
    Zen strawberry orange
        smoothie 123
smoothoccino 123
snapper in a yogurt coat 206
sole: steamed duo of sole and
        halibut with rainbow
        pepper stir-fry 216
soups: cauliflower-almond-
        garlic soup 160
    celery root and mushroom
        soup 150
    cool and spicy tomato
        soup 71
    to freeze 70

iced gazpacho 176
Silicon Valley spilt pea
soup 179
Southwestern spice rub 63
Spanish rice 221
spice rub, Southwestern 63
spices, to toast and grind 63
spicy tomato-celery-lime 35
spinach: farfalle with tuna,
wilted spinach, sun-dried
tomatoes, and pine
nuts 223
filet mignon with crisp
bacon, seared polenta,
and wilted spinach
salad 210
Santa Barbara salad 185
spinach latkes 239
summer vegan spinach
salad 166
tofu with spinach and
chilies 217
split pea soup, Silicon Valley
179
spring rolls, Khmer 148
steamed duo of sole and
halibut with rainbow
pepper stir-fry 216
stock 92
to freeze 70
summer vegan spinach
salad 166
super-simple awesome fish
tacos 171
sushi, seitan or Quorn
cabbage 226
sweet potato biscuits 243

III: T
tacos, breakfast 131
super-simple awesome
fish 171
tartlets, smoked salmon 244
Thai forbidden rice salad 229
three-melon crush 35
toasted sesame oil 48

tofu: Chinese tofu salad 168
Khmer spring rolls 148
tofu niçoise 227
tofu with spinach and
chilies 217
tomatoes: heirloom tomato
and baby leaf salad 152
iced gazpacho 176
spicy tomato-celery-lime 35
tomato-basil cubes 69
vine-ripe tomato and
buffalo mozzarella with
marinated beets and
arugula salad 157
tortelloni with creamy fava
beans and thyme 218
tuna: farfalle with tuna, wilted
spinach, sun-dried
tomatoes, and pine nuts
223
peppered tuna carpaccio
155
raw 36, 37
seared Southwestern ahi
tuna tornadoes 188
turkey-avocado-carrot wrap
151

III: V
vanilla-infused vinegar 45
vegetables: to freeze 66
homegrown 99
raw 30
vinaigrettes 46
vine-ripe tomato and buffalo
mozzarella with
marinated beets and
arugula salad 157
vinegar, chili-infused 61
vanilla-infused 45
vinegars 43–45

III: W
wake-up breakfast smoothie
121
wake-up shake-me-up power

shake 118
wasabi vinaigrette 46
Washington nutty-blue
smoothie 120
watermelon saté with honey-
vinegar dipping sauce
wheatgrass 31
wholegrain and berry salad,
mixed 173
wild salmon and warm beet
salad 221
wine vinegar 45
wrap, banana-peanut butter
232
smoked salmon–sun-dried
cranberries–goat cheese
236
turkey-avocado-carrot 151

III: Y
yogurt 80
apple–yogurt–almonds 234
black and blue yogurt
fru fru 108

III: Z
Zen strawberry-orange
smoothie 123

SOURCES

//
> Sriracha Hot Chilli Sauce is available in most Asian markets and even some mainstream supermarket chains. See www.hoohing.com
//
> The Three Crabs brand of fish sauce is available in most Asian markets.
//
> Kewpie mayonnaise is available in Asian markets and online.
See www.japancentre.com
//
> To find fennel pollen for cheese-flavoured oil, try www.fennelpollen.com or www.thespiceshop.co.uk
//
> Kamut, farro, and other grains, are sold at Whole Foods markets. You can also find grits there.
//
> For advice on fish from sustainable sources log on to www.msc.org
//

ACKNOWLEDGMENTS

// To my wife and son for putting up with me and all the late-night cooking, testing of recipes, endless hours of research, and photo shoots, and for allowing the media into our home on a moment's notice. Thank you Kimmie for all the love and support you show me in my many projects that often end up dragging you in as well.

// To my parents and brother for supporting me, even when we all thought this path I had decided to travel in life would never pay off. Thank you for having faith and believing in my abilities, and helping me to pursue my dreams of becoming a chef.

// To Larry Page and Sergey Brin for taking a leap of faith in bringing me in as Google's very first executive chef. Thank you for allowing me to grow with your company and be part of your world. Many times I felt like Homer Simpson around the two of you. Thank you George Salah for actually being the guy at Google to hire me, relating to me as well as you could, and for encouraging me to create a really special experience for the Googlers every day. Thank you Jim Glass and the Google Culinary Team for being such a great kick ass group of people – you know who you are.

// To the entire Google family – to everyone who ever had the courage to ring the bell when we weren't open yet, to all who ever volunteered to work in the café when I was shorthanded, and to those who contributed recipes they thought would be appreciated. (Were they surprised when I served them! Of course I tweaked them slightly.) And to all the extended Google family that would volunteer to help out with big celebration meals and events, Hanukkah, Chinese New Year, and Big Ass BBQs.

// To the Marin & Sonoma County Crew for believing in me and supporting me through the years. To all the chefs and restaurateurs I ever worked under who taught me what to do and what not to do. To all the vendors who have taken care of me over the years. Special thanks to Steve Kimock, Chef Cat Cora, Chef Ming Tsai, Chef Ken Orringer, David Vise, and Karen Alexander, for the kind words, great food, and amazing music. Thank you to the legal team at Wilson, Sonsini Goodrich & Rosati.

// To Nuba Bear of Three Captains Sea Products, Half Moon Bay, CA; Dee Harley of Harley Farms Goat Dairy, Pescadero, CA, Phipps Country Farm, Pescadero, CA; The Wild Butcher at Dittmer's Gourmet Meats and Wurst-Haus, Mountain View, CA; Sigona's Farmer's Market in Redwood City, CA; San Francisco Ferry Plaza Farmers' Market; Fairfax Farmer's Market, Fairfax, CA; Whole Foods Markets; Trader Joe's; Cowgirl Creamery; Bassian Farms; Sky Vodka; Anchor Steam Brewery; and Vegiworks.

// To the kind folks over at DK for giving me the opportunity to create this cookbook. To the creative team over at Smith & Gilmour in the UK. To Noel Murphy Photography. Thanks to Alex and Noel for being able to hang with me for a couple of days in the States and drink some local beer.

// To all the artists and musicians in my life for allowing me to share in your world. Without you, life would be so boring.

// To Al Gore for caring about the planet. To Howard Cohen. To God for helping me get this done. Most importantly, Thank You for buying this book.

// A portion of the proceeds from this book will be donated to charity.

100

things you should know about

BIRDS

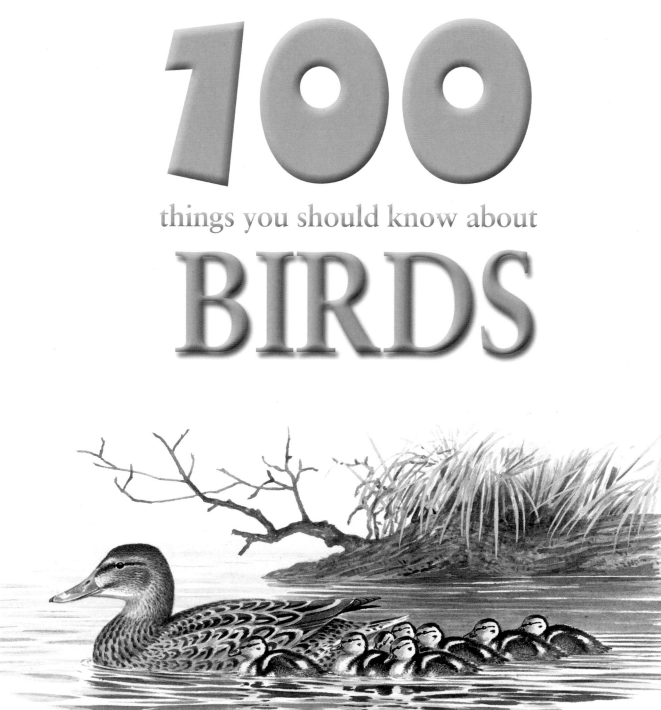

100

things you should know about

BIRDS

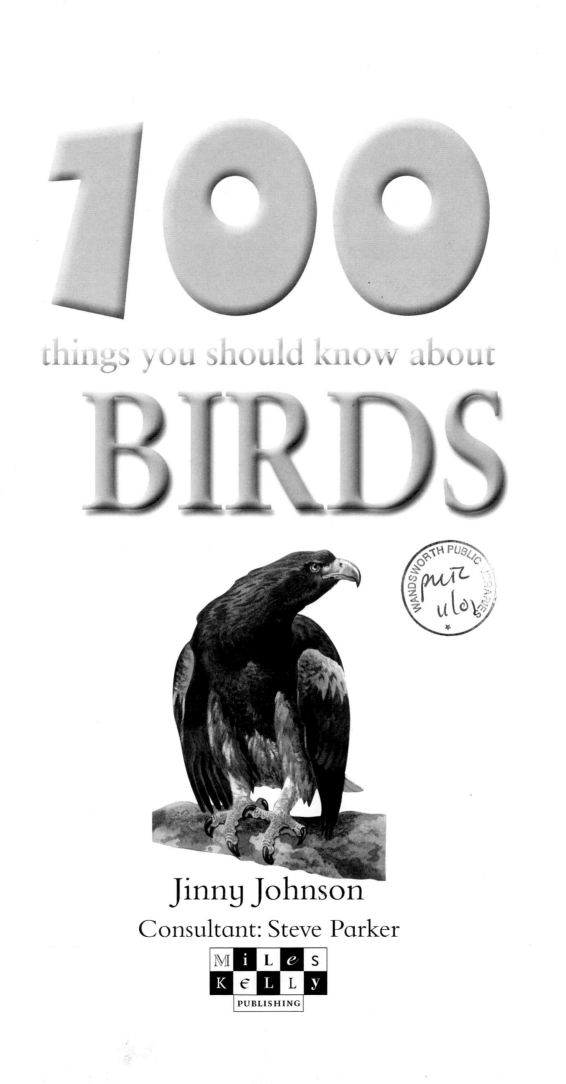

Jinny Johnson

Consultant: Steve Parker

Miles
Kelly
PUBLISHING

First published in 2001 by
Miles Kelly Publishing Ltd
Bardfield Centre, Great Bardfield, Essex, CM7 4SL

Copyright © Miles Kelly Publishing 2001

2 4 6 8 10 9 7 5 3 1

Editorial Director: Paula Borton
Art Director: Clare Sleven
Project Editor, Copy Editor: Neil de Cort
Editorial Assistant: Nicola Sail
Designer: Sally Lace
Artwork Commissioning: Janice Bracken
Picture Research: Lesley Cartlidge and Liberty Newton
Proof Reading, Indexing: Janet De Saulles

500 646916

ISBN 1-84236-008-6

Printed in Hong Kong

ACKNOWLEDGEMENTS
The Publishers would like to thank the following artists who have
contributed to this book:

Chris Buzer/ Studio Galante
Luca Di Castri/ Studio Galante
Jim Channell/ Bernard Thornton
Illustration
Mike Foster/ Maltings Partnership
L.R. Galante/ Studio Galante
Terry Gabbey/ AFA
Roger Gorringe
Brooks Hagan/ Studio Galante

Alan Harris
Roger Kent
Kevin Maddison
Janos Marffy
Massimiliano Maugeri/ Studio Galante
Eric Robson/ Illustration Limited
Francesco Spadoni/ Studio Galante
Rudi Vizi
Mike White/ Temple Rogers

Cartoons by Mark Davis at Mackerel

www.mileskelly.net
info@mileskelly.net

Contents

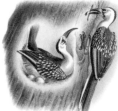

What are birds? 6

The bird world 8

Big and small 10

Fast movers 12

Superb swimmers 14

Looking good! 16

Night birds 18

Home sweet home 20

Great travellers 22

Desert dwellers 24

Staying safe 26

Safe and sound 28

Deadly hunters 30

Caring for the young 32

Deep in the jungle 34

The biggest birds 36

Messing about in the river 38

Can I have some more? 40

Life in snow and ice 42

Special beaks 44

Birds and people 46

Index 48

What are birds?

1 **A bird has two legs, a pair of wings and a body that is covered with feathers.** Birds are, perhaps, the animals we see most often in the wild. They live all over the world – everywhere from Antarctica to the hottest deserts and rainforests. They range in size from the huge ostrich, which stands 2.75 metres tall, a whole metre taller than a man, to the tiny bee hummingbird, which is scarcely bigger than a real bee.

Osprey

Greater flamingo

Grey heron

Mallard

Kingfisher

Greater honeyguide

Helmeted hornbill

Masai ostrich

Red-billed hornbill

Blue peafowl

Lesser green broadbill

African jacana

Blue-crowned hanging parrot

7

The bird world

2 **There are more than 9000 different types, or species, of bird.** These have been organized by scientists into groups called orders which contain many different species. The largest order is called the passerines, also known as perching or song birds. These include common birds such as robins.

Crown

Bill, or beak

Throat

Flight feathers

Light, hollow bones, or skeleton

Kidney

Lung

Heart

Liver

Stomach

Tail feathers

Toes

▲ Most doves and pigeons are hunted by predators. Strong wing muscles, that make up a third of their weight, help them to take off rapidly and accelerate to 80 kilometres an hour.

3 **Birds are the only creatures that have feathers.** The feathers are made of keratin – the same material as our hair and nails. Feathers keep a bird warm and protect it from the wind and rain. Its wing and tail feathers allow a bird to fly. Some birds also have very colourful feathers which help them to attract mates or blend in with their surroundings. This is called camouflage.

▶ The bird with the most feathers is thought to be the whistling swan, with more than 25,000 feathers.

4 **All birds have wings.** These are the bird's front limbs. There are many different wing shapes. Birds that soar in the sky for hours, such as hawks and eagles, have long broad wings. These allow them to make the best use of air currents. Small fast-flying birds such as swifts have slim, pointed wings.

► The egg protects the growing young and provides it with food. While the young develops the parent birds, such as this song thrush, keep the egg safe and warm.

5   **All birds lay eggs.** It would be impossible for birds to carry their developing young inside their bodies like mammals do – they would become too heavy to fly.

6   **All birds have a beak for eating.** The beak is made of bone and is covered with a hard material called horn. Birds have different kinds of beak for different types of food. Insect-eating birds tend to have thin, sharp beaks for picking up their tiny prey. The short, strong parrot's beak is ideal for cracking hard-shelled nuts.

QUIZ

1. How many types of bird are there?
2. How many feathers does the whistling swan have?
3. What are feathers made of?
4. What is the largest order of birds called?
5. What sort of beaks do hunting birds have?

1. More than 9000
2. More than 25,000 3. Keratin
4. The passerines
5. Powerful hooked beaks

◄ Hunting birds, such as this goshawk, have powerful hooked beaks for tearing flesh.

Big and small

7 **The world's largest bird is the ostrich.** This long-legged bird stands up to 2.75 metres tall and weighs up to 115 kilograms – twice as much as an average adult human. Males are slightly larger than females. The ostrich lives on the grasslands of Africa where it feeds on plant material such as leaves, flowers and seeds.

▼ The great bustard lives in southern Europe and parts of Asia.

8 **The heaviest flying bird is the great bustard.** The male is up to 1 metre long and weighs about 18 kilograms, although the female is slightly smaller. The bustard is a strong flier, but it does spend much of its life on the ground, walking or running on its strong legs.

▼ A bee hummingbird, life size!

9 **The bee hummingbird is the world's smallest bird.** Its body, including its tail, is only about 5 centimetres long and it weighs only 2 grams – about the same as a small spoonful of rice. It lives on Caribbean islands and, like other hummingbirds, feeds on flower nectar.

10 **The largest bird of prey is the Andean condor.** A type of vulture, this bird measures about 110 centimetres long and weighs up to 12 kilograms. This huge bird of prey soars over the Andes Mountains of South America, hunting for food.

▼ Like most vultures, the condor is a scavenger. It looks for carrion, the carcasses of dead animals and the remains of other hunters' kills.

11 The wandering albatross has the longest wings of any bird. When outstretched, they measure as much as 3.3 metres from tip to tip. The albatross spends most of its life in the air. It flies over the oceans, searching for fish and squid which it snatches from the water surface.

◄ The wandering albatross only comes to land at breeding time. It lays its eggs on islands in the South Pacific, South Atlantic and Indian Ocean.

QUIZ

1. How much does a bee hummingbird weigh?
2. Where do ostriches live?
3. What does the great bustard eat?
4. How long are the wandering albatross's wings?
5. Where does the collared falconet live?

1. 2 grams 2. Africa 3. Insects and seeds 4. 3.3 metres from tip to tip 5. India and Southeast Asia

12 Wilson's storm petrel is the smallest seabird in the world. Only 16 to 19 centimetres long, this petrel hops over the water surface snatching up tiny sea creatures to eat. It is very common over the Atlantic, Indian and Antarctic Oceans.

13 The smallest bird of prey is the collared falconet. This little bird, which lives in India and Southeast Asia, is only about 19 centimetres long. It hunts insects and other small birds.

Fast movers

14 **The fastest flying bird is the peregrine falcon.** It hunts other birds in the air and makes spectacular high-speed dives to catch its prey. During a hunting dive, a peregrine may move as fast as 180 kilometres an hour. In normal level flight, it flies at about 95 kilometres an hour. Peregrine falcons live almost all over the world.

15 **Ducks and geese are also fast fliers.** Many of them can fly at speeds of more than 65 kilometres an hour. The red-breasted merganser and the common eider duck can fly at up to 100 kilometres an hour.

▼ Sword-billed hummingbird

When this hummingbird lands, it has to tilt its head right back to support the weight of its huge bill.

Tail feathers spread for landing.

16 **A hummingbird's wings beat 50 or more times a second as it hovers in the air.** The tiny bee hummingbird may beat its wings at an amazing 200 times a second. When hovering, the hummingbird holds its body upright and beats its wings backwards and forwards, not up and down, to keep itself in one place in the air. The fast-beating wings make a low buzzing or humming sound that gives these birds their name.

◀ The peregrine falcon does not just fold its wings and fall like many birds, it actually pushes itself down towards the ground. This powered dive is called a stoop.

FEED THE BIRDS!

In winter, food can be scarce for birds. You can make your own food cake to help them.

You will need:
225g of suet, lard or dripping
500g of seeds, nuts, biscuit crumbs, cake and other scraps

Ask an adult for help. First melt the fat, and mix it thoroughly with the seed and scraps. Pour it into an old yogurt pot or similar container, and leave it to cool and harden. Remove the cake from the container. Make a hole through the cake, put a string through the hole and hang it from a tree outside.

17 The swift spends nearly all its life in the air and rarely comes to land. It can catch prey, eat, drink and mate on the wing. After leaving its nest, a young swift may not come to land again for two years, and may fly as far as 500,000 kilometres.

18 The greater roadrunner is a fast mover on land. It runs at speeds of 20 kilometres an hour as it hunts for insects, lizards and birds' eggs to eat. It can fly but seems generally to prefer running.

Swifts eat insects which they chase and catch in mid-air!

◀ The spine-tailed swift is thought to fly at speeds of up to 160 kilometres an hour.

Swifts have long, slim wings that are perfect for their life in the air.

Superb swimmers

19 Penguins are the best swimmers and divers in the bird world. They live in and around the Antarctic, which is right at the very south of the world. They spend most of their lives in water, where they catch fish and tiny animals called krill to eat, but they do come to land to breed. Their wings act as strong flippers to push them through the water, and their tail and webbed feet help them steer. Penguins sometimes get around on land by tobogganing over ice on their tummies!

Emperor penguin

20 The gentoo penguin is one of the fastest swimming birds. It can swim at up to 27 kilometres an hour — that's faster than most people can run! Mostly, though, penguins probably swim at about 5 to 10 kilometres an hour.

21

The gannet makes an amazing dive from a height of 30 metres above the sea to catch fish in the sea. This seabird spots its prey as it soars above the ocean. Then with wings swept back and neck and beak held straight out in front, the gannet plunges like a dive-bomber. It enters the water, seizes its prey and surfaces a few seconds later.

Northern gannet

QUIZ

1. From how high does a gannet dive?
2. How many kinds of penguin are there?
3. How fast can a gentoo penguin swim?
4. How long can an emperor penguin stay underwater?
5. Where do most kinds of penguin live?

1. 30 metres
2. 18 3. 27 kilometres an hour
4. 18 minutes 5. Antarctica

▼ King penguins and emperor penguins regularly dive deeper than 250 metres. Emperor penguins have been timed making dives lasting more than 18 minutes.

King penguin

◄ There are about 18 different kinds of penguin. Most live in and around Antarctica.

Looking good!

22 At the start of the breeding season male birds try to attract females. Some do this by showing off their beautiful feathers. Others perform special displays or dances. The male peacock has a long train of colourful feathers. When female birds come near, he begins to spread his tail, showing off the beautiful eye-like markings. He dances up and down and shivers the feathers to get the females' attention.

23 The male bowerbird attracts a mate by making a structure of twigs called a bower. The bird spends many hours making it attractive, by decorating it with berries and flowers. Females choose the males with the prettiest bowers. After mating, the female goes away and makes a nest for her eggs. The male's bower is no longer needed.

24 The male roller performs a special display flight to impress his mate. Starting high in the air, he tumbles and rolls down to the ground while the female watches from a perch. Rollers are brightly coloured insect-eating birds that live in Africa, Europe, Asia and Australia.

Spotted bowerbird

Fawn breasted bowerbird

Black faced golden bowerbird

◀ Bowerbirds live in Australia and New Guinea.

▼ Female peacocks tend to choose the males with the most attractive feathers.

I DON'T BELIEVE IT!

Water birds called great crested grebes perform a courtship dance together. During the dance they offer each other gifts – beakfuls of water weed!

Cock-of-the-rock

25 The blue bird of paradise hangs upside-down to show off his wonderful feathers. As he hangs, his tail feathers spread out and he swings backwards and forwards while making a special call to attract the attention of female birds. Most birds of paradise live in New Guinea. All the males have beautiful plumage, but females are much plainer.

26 Male cock-of-the-rock dance to attract mates. Some of the most brightly coloured birds in the world, they gather in groups and leap up and down to show off their plumage to admiring females. They live in the South American rainforest.

27 The nightingale sings its tuneful song to attract females. Courtship is the main reason why birds sing, although some may sing at other times of year. A female nightingale chooses a male for his song rather than his looks.

Night birds

28 Some birds, such as the poorwill, hunt insects at night when there is less competition for prey. The poorwill sleeps during the day and wakes up at dusk to start hunting. As it flies, it opens its beak very wide and snaps moths out of the air.

▲ As well as moths, the poorwill also catches grasshoppers and beetles on the ground.

30 The kakapo is the only parrot that is active at night. It is also a ground-living bird. All other parrots are daytime birds that live in and around trees. During the day the kakapo sleeps in a burrow or under a rock, and at night it comes out to find fruit, berries and leaves to eat. It cannot fly, but it can climb up into trees using its beak and feet. The kakapo only lives in New Zealand.

29 The barn owl is perfectly adapted for night-time hunting. Its eyes are very large and sensitive to the dimmest light. Its ears can pinpoint the tiniest sound and help it to locate prey. Most feathers make a sound as they cut through the air, but the fluffy edges of the owl's feathers soften the sound of wing beats so the owl can swoop silently on its prey.

Kakapo

31

Like bats, the oilbird uses sounds to help it fly in darkness. As it flies, it makes clicking noises which bounce off objects in the caves in South America where it lives, and help the bird find its way. At night, the oilbird leaves its cave to feed on the fruits of palm trees.

32

Unlike most birds, the kiwi has a good sense of smell which helps it find food at night. Using the nostrils at the tip of its long beak, the kiwi sniffs out worms and other creatures hiding in the soil. It plunges its beak into the ground to reach its prey.

Kiwi

QUIZ

1. Where are the kiwi's nostrils?
2. Where does the kakapo live?
3. What does the oilbird eat?
4. What's special about the barn owl's feathers?
5. What kind of bird is a poorwill?

1. At the end of its beak
2. New Zealand 3. The fruits of palm trees
4. They have fluffy edges
5. It is a type of nightjar

Home sweet home

33 Birds make nests in which to lay their eggs and keep them safe. The bald eagle makes one of the biggest nests of any bird. The nest is made of sticks and is built in a tall tree or on rocks. It is used year after year. It can grow as large as 2.5 metres across and 3.5 metres deep — big enough for several people to get into!

34 The female hornbill lays her eggs in prison! The male hornbill walls up his mate and her eggs in a tree hole. He blocks the entrance to the hole with mud, leaving only a small opening. The female looks after the eggs and the male brings food, passing it through the opening. Once the eggs hatch the female has to remain safely in the hole with her young for a few weeks while the male supplies food.

▲ The bald eagle lives in North America. In 1782 the United States adopted the bald eagle as its national bird.

The male weaver bird twists strips of leaves around a branch or twig.

35 **The male weaver bird makes a nest from grass and stems.** He knots and weaves the pieces together to make a long nest, which hangs from the branch of a tree. The nest makes a warm, cosy home for the eggs and young, and is also very hard for any predator to get into.

Then, he makes a roof, and an entrance so he can get inside!

When it's finished, the long entrance helps to provide a safe shelter for the eggs.

36 **The cave swiftlet makes a nest from its own saliva or spit.** It uses the spit as glue to make a cup-shaped nest of feathers and grass.

37 **The mallee fowl makes a temperature-controlled nest mound.** It is made of plants covered with sand. As the plants rot, the inside of the mound gets warmer. The female bird lays her eggs in holes made in the sides of the mound. The male bird then keeps a check on the temperature with his beak. If the mound cools, he adds more sand. If it gets too hot he makes some openings to let warmth out.

Mallee fowl

38 **The cuckoo doesn't make a nest at all – she lays her eggs in the nests of other birds!** She lays up to 12 eggs, all in different nests. The owner of the nest is called the host bird. The female cuckoo removes one of the host bird's eggs before she puts one of her own in, so the number in the nest remains the same.

I DON'T BELIEVE IT!

Most birds take several minutes to lay an egg. The cuckoo can lay her egg in 9 seconds! This allows her to pop her egg into a nest while the owner's back is turned.

Great travellers

39 The Canada goose spends the summer in the Arctic and flies south in winter. This regular journey is called a migration. In summer, the Arctic bursts into bloom and there are plenty of plants for the geese to eat while they lay their eggs and rear their young. In autumn, when the weather turns cold, they migrate, this means they leave to fly to warmer climates farther south. This means that the bird gets warmer weather all year round.

▼ The Canada goose tends to return to its birthplace to breed.

▶ The Arctic tern travels farther than any other bird and sees more hours of daylight each year than any other creature.

40 The Arctic tern makes one of the longest migrations of any bird. It breeds in the Arctic during the northern summer. Then, as the northern winter approaches, the tern makes the long journey south to the Antarctic – a trip of some 15,000 kilometres – where it catches the southern summer. In this way the tern gets the benefit of long daylight hours for feeding all year round.

◀ The American golden plover is camouflaged in the tundra vegetation by the spectacular patterns on its back.

41 Every autumn, the American golden plover flies up to 12,800 kilometres from North to South America. It breeds on the North American tundra where it feasts on the insects that fill the air during the brief Arctic summer. When summer is over the plover flies to South America for the winter. This means it has plentiful food supplies all year round.

WHO GOES WHERE?

On this world map are the migration routes of the Canada goose, the Arctic tern and the American golden plover. Each one is a different colour. Can you work out which is which?

Yellow: Canada goose
Red: Arctic tern
Green: American golden plover.

23

Desert dwellers

42 **Many desert birds have sandy-brown feathers to blend with their surroundings.** This helps them hide from their enemies. The cream-coloured courser lives in desert lands in Africa and parts of Asia. It is hard to see on the ground, but when it flies, the black and white pattern on its wings makes it more obvious. So the courser runs around rather than fly. It feeds on insects and other creatures it digs from the desert sands.

▲ Cream-coloured courser

▶ The elf owl is able to catch prey in its feet as it flies.

44 **The elf owl makes its nest in a hole in a desert cactus.** This prickly, uncomfortable home helps to keep the owl's eggs safe from enemies, who do not want to struggle through the cactus' spines. The elf owl is one of the smallest owls in the world and is only about 14 centimetres long. It lives in desert areas in the southwest of the USA.

43 **Birds may have to travel long distances to find water in the desert.** But this is not always possible for little chicks. To solve this problem, the male sandgrouse has special feathers on his tummy which act like sponges to hold water. He flies off to find water and thoroughly soaks his feathers. He then returns home where his young thirstily gulp down the water that he's brought.

▶ The sandgrouse lives throughout Asia, often in semi-desert areas.

45

The cactus wren eats cactus fruits and berries. This little bird hops about among the spines of cactus plants and takes any juicy morsels it can find. It also catches insects, small lizards and frogs on the ground. Cactus wrens live in the southwestern USA.

46

The lappet-faced vulture scavenges for its food. It glides over the deserts of Africa and the Middle East, searching for dead animals or the left-overs of hunters such as lions. When it spots something, the vulture swoops down and attacks the carcass with its strong hooked bill. Its head and neck are bare so it does not have to spend time cleaning its feathers after feeding from a messy carcass.

▼ The lappet-faced vulture has very broad wings. These are ideal for soaring high above the plains of its African home, searching for food.

Staying safe

47 **Birds have clever ways of hiding themselves from enemies.** The tawny frogmouth is an Australian bird that hunts at night. During the day, it rests in a tree where its brownish, mottled feathers make it hard to see. If the bird senses danger it stretches itself, with its beak pointing upwards, so that it looks almost exactly like an old broken branch or tree stump.

Tawny frogmouth

48 **If a predator comes too close to her nest and young, the female killdeer leads the enemy away by a clever trick.** She moves away from the nest, which is made on the ground, making sure the predator has noticed her. She then starts to drag one wing as though she is injured and is easy prey. When she has led the predator far enough away from her young she suddenly flies up into the air and escapes.

▶ The killdeer lives in North America.

49 Guillemots find that there is safety in numbers. Thousands of these birds live together on cliff tops and rocks. They do not build nests but simply lay their eggs on the rock or bare earth. Most land hunters cannot reach the birds on these rocks, and any flying egg thieves are soon driven away by the mass of screeching, pecking birds.

I DON'T BELIEVE IT!

The guillemot's egg is pear-shaped with one end much more pointed than the other. This means that the egg rolls round in a circle if it is pushed or knocked, so does not fall off the cliff.

Safe and sound

50 **A bird's egg protects the developing chick inside.** The yellow yolk in the egg provides the baby bird with food while it is growing. Layers of egg white, called albumen, cushion the chick and keep it warm, while the hard shell keeps everything safe. The shell is porous – it allows air in and out so that the chick can breathe. The parent birds keep the egg warm in a nest. This is called incubation.

1. The chick starts to chip away at the egg.

53 **The kiwi lays an egg a quarter of her own size.** The egg weighs 420 grams – the kiwi only weighs 1.7 kilograms. This is like a new baby weighing 17.5 kilograms, most weigh about 3.5 kilograms.

51 **The biggest egg in the world is laid by the ostrich.** An ostrich egg weighs about 1.5 kilograms – an average hen's egg weighs only about 50 grams. The shell of the ostrich egg is very strong, measuring up to 2 millimetres thick.

52 **The smallest egg in the world is laid by the bee hummingbird.** It weighs about 0.3 grams. The bird itself weighs only 2 grams.

Ostrich egg

Bee hummingbird egg

4. The chick is able to wriggle free. Its parents will look after it for several weeks until it can look after itself.

2. The chick uses its egg tooth to break free.

3. The egg splits wide open.

54 The number of eggs laid in a clutch varies from 1 to more than 20. A clutch is the name for the number of eggs that a bird lays in one go. The number of clutches per year also changes from bird to bird. The grey partridge lays one of the biggest clutches, with an average of 15 to 19 eggs, and the common turkey usually lays 10 to 15 eggs. The emperor penguin lays one egg a year.

▲ Common turkey

QUIZ

1. How thick is the shell of an ostrich egg?
2. How many eggs a year does the emperor penguin lay?
3. How much does the bee hummingbird's egg weigh?
4. For how long does the wandering albatross incubate its eggs?
5. For how long does the great spotted woodpecker incubate its eggs?

1. 2 millimetres 2. One 3. 0.3 grams 4. up to 82 days 5. 10 days

55 The great spotted woodpecker incubates its egg for only 10 days. This is one of the shortest incubation periods of any bird. The longest incubation period is of the wandering albatross, which incubates its eggs for up to 82 days.

Deadly hunters

56 The golden eagle is one of the fiercest hunters of all birds. The eagle has extremely keen eyesight and can see objects from a far greater distance than humans can manage. When it spies a victim, the eagle dives down and seizes its prey in its powerful talons. It then rips the flesh apart with its strong hooked beak. The golden eagle usually has two eggs. However, the first chick to hatch often kills the younger chick. Golden eagles live in North America, Europe, North Africa and Asia.

Steller's sea eagle

57 The sea eagle feeds on fish that it snatches from the water surface. The eagle soars over the ocean searching for signs of prey. It swoops down, seizes a fish in its sharp claws and flies off to a rock or cliff to eat its meal. Spikes on the soles of the eagle's feet help it hold onto its slippery prey. Other eagles have special prey, too. The snake eagle feeds mostly on snakes and lizards. It has short, rough-surfaced toes that help it grip its prey.

▼ The golden eagle can soar for hours on its huge wings, searching for prey such as rabbits and other birds.

I DON'T BELIEVE IT!

Eagles like to make their nests in high places. One pair of sea eagles made their nest on top of a tall navigation beacon on the coast of Norway.

58 **The raven is the biggest of all the songbirds and a powerful hunter.** It grows up to 63 centimetres long, it has a strong, hooked beak for attacking its victims and it can run fast on the ground as well as fly when chasing prey. Rats and mice are its main catches, but it steals other birds' eggs and can even kill a creature as large as a rabbit. Ravens also scavenge for food, taking animals that are already dead or the remains of the kills of other hunters.

▶ Ravens live in North America, Europe, and parts of Africa and Asia.

Caring for the young

59 Emperor penguins have the worst breeding conditions of any bird. They lay eggs and rear their young on the Antarctic ice. The female penguin lays one egg at the start of the Antarctic winter. She returns to the sea, leaving her partner to incubate the egg on his feet. The egg is covered by a flap of the father's skin and feathers – so it is much warmer than the surroundings.

▲ While the male penguin incubates the egg he does not eat. When the chick hatches, the female returns to take over its care while the exhausted, hungry male finds food.

60 Pigeons feed their young on 'pigeon milk'. This special liquid is made in the lining of part of the bird's throat, called the crop. The young birds are fed on this for the first few days of their life and then start to eat seeds and other solid food.

61 Hawks and falcons care for their young and bring them food for many weeks. Their chicks are born blind and helpless. They are totally dependent on their parents for food and protection until they grow large enough to hunt for themselves.

▶ A sparrowhawk and her chicks.

A mallard, a type of duck, with her ducklings.

62 Other birds, such as ducks and geese, are able to run around and find food as soon as they hatch. Baby ducks follow the first moving thing they see when they hatch – usually their mother. This reaction is called imprinting. It is a form of very rapid learning that can happen only in the first few hours of an animal's life. Imprinting ensures that the young birds stay close to their mother and do not wander away.

I DON'T BELIEVE IT!

While male penguins incubate their eggs they huddle together for warmth. The birds take it in turns to stand on the outside and take the force of the freezing winds.

63 Swans carry their young on their back as they swim. This allows the parent bird to move fast without having to wait for the young, called cygnets, to keep up. When the cygnets are riding on the parent bird's back they are safe from enemies.

64 Young birds must learn their songs from adults. A young bird such as a chaffinch is born being able to make sounds. But, like a human baby learning to speak, it has to learn the chaffinch song by listening to its parents and practising.

Deep in the jungle

Harpy eagle

65 Birds of paradise are among the most colourful of all rainforest birds. Only the males have brilliant plumage and decorative feathers; the females are generally much plainer. There are about 42 different kinds of birds of paradise and they all live in the rainforests of New Guinea and northeast Australia. Fruit is their main food but some also feed on insects and spiders.

66 The Congo peafowl was only discovered in 1936. It lives in the dense rainforest of West Africa and has rarely been seen. The male bird has beautiful glossy feathers while the female is mostly brown and black.

Hoatzin

Congo peafowl

67 The harpy eagle is the world's largest eagle. It is about 90 centimetres long and has huge feet and long sharp claws. It feeds on rainforest animals such as monkeys and sloths, which it catches in the trees.

68 The hoatzin builds its nest overhanging water. If its chicks are in danger they can escape by dropping into the water and swimming to safety. This strange bird with its ragged crest lives in the Amazon rainforest in South America.

69 The quetzal has magnificent tail feathers which are up to 90 centimetres long. This beautiful bird lives in the rainforests of Central America. It was worshipped as a sacred bird by the ancient Mayan and Aztec people.

Quetzal

Scarlet macaw

Junglefowl

QUIZ

1. When was the Congo peafowl discovered?
2. How long are the quetzal's tail feathers?
3. How many kinds of birds of paradise are there?
4. Where does the scarlet macaw live?
5. How do the hoatzin's chicks escape danger?

1. 1936 2. About 90 centimetres 3. About 42 4. South America 5. They drop out of their nest into the water

70 The scarlet macaw is one of the largest parrots in the world. This spectacular bird is 85 centimetres long, including its very long tail and lives in the South American rainforest. It moves in flocks of 20 or so that screech loudly as they fly from tree to tree feeding on fruit and leaves.

71 The junglefowl is the ancestor of the farmyard chicken. This colourful bird lives in the Southeast Asian rainforest, where it feeds on seeds and insects.

The biggest birds

72 The fast-running emu is the largest bird in Australia. Like the ostrich it cannot fly, but it can run at speeds of more than 50 kilometres an hour on its long legs as it searches for fruit, berries and insects to eat. In the breeding season the female lays up to 10 eggs in a dip in the ground. The male then takes over and incubates the clutch.

▼ The ostrich is the world's fastest two-legged runner. It is specially adapted for speed, and can run at up to 70 kilometres an hour.

Very powerful upper leg muscles

Extra flexible knees

Long, strong legs

Bendy two-toed feet

▼ These flightless birds are among the largest birds in the world.

Emu

Kiwi

73

The rhea lives on the grassy plains of South America. It is a fast-running bird but it cannot fly. It eats mainly grass and other small plants, but it also catches insects and other small creatures such as lizards. In the breeding season, male rheas fight to gather a flock of females. Once he has his flock, the male rhea digs a nest in the ground. Each of the females lays her eggs in this nest. The male incubates the eggs, and he looks after the chicks until they are about six months old.

▼ The rhea can sprint faster than a horse, reaching speeds of up to 50 kilometres an hour.

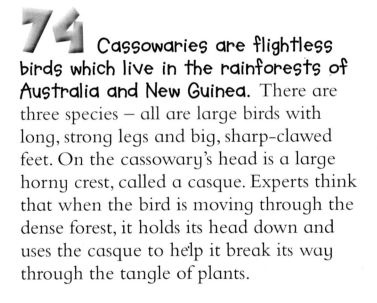

Cassowary

74

Cassowaries are flightless birds which live in the rainforests of Australia and New Guinea. There are three species – all are large birds with long, strong legs and big, sharp-clawed feet. On the cassowary's head is a large horny crest, called a casque. Experts think that when the bird is moving through the dense forest, it holds its head down and uses the casque to help it break its way through the tangle of plants.

I DON'T BELIEVE IT!

One rhea egg is the equivalent to about 12 hen's eggs. It has long been a tasty feast for local people.

Messing about in the river

75 The jacana can walk on water! It has amazingly long toes that spread the bird's weight over a large area and allow it to walk on floating lily pads as it hunts for food such as insects and seeds. Jacanas can also swim and dive. There are eight different types of jacana, also called lilytrotters. They live in parts of North and South America, Africa and Asia.

76 The kingfisher makes its nest in a tunnel in a riverbank. Using their strong beaks, a male and female pair dig a tunnel up to 60 centimetres long and make a nesting chamber at the end. The female lays up to eight eggs which both parents take turns to look after.

77 The heron catches fish and other water creatures. This long-legged bird stands on the shore or in shallow water and reaches forward to grab its prey with a swift thrust of its dagger-like beak.

78 A small bird called the dipper is well-adapted to river life. It usually lives around fast-flowing streams and can swim and dive well. It can even walk along the bottom of a stream, snapping up prey such as insects and other small creatures. There are five different types of dipper and they live in North and South America, Asia and Europe.

79 The pelican collects fish in the big pouch that hangs beneath its long beak. When the pelican pushes its beak into the water the pouch stretches and fills with water – and fish. When the pelican then lifts its head up, the water drains out of the pouch leaving any food behind.

The pelican uses its pouch like a net to catch fish.

80 The osprey is a bird of prey which feeds mainly on fish. This bird is found nearly all over the world near rivers and lakes. It watches for prey from the air then plunges into the water with its feet held out in front ready to grab a fish. Special spikes on the soles of its feet help it hold onto its slippery catch.

Can I have some more?

81 The woodpecker uses its special strong beak to bore into tree trunks and catch insects. The bird holds on tightly to a tree trunk with the help of its strong feet and sharp claws. Its stiff tail feathers also help to give it support. It starts to hammer into the trunk, disturbing wood-boring insects that live beneath the tree bark. The insects try to flee, but the woodpecker quickly snaps them up.

▶ There are more than 200 different kinds of woodpecker, including this Eurasian woodpecker. They live in North and South America, Africa, Europe and Asia.

82

The antbird keeps watch over army ants as they march through the forest. The bird flies just ahead of the ants and perches on a low branch. It then pounces on the many insects, spiders and other small creatures that try to escape from the marching column of ants. Some antbirds also eat the ants themselves. There are about 240 different types of antbirds that live in Central and South America.

▼ Honeyguides have been known to lead honey-loving humans to bees' nests.

84

The honeyguide bird uses the honey badger to help it get food. The honeyguide feeds on bee grubs and honey. It can find the bees' nests but it is not strong enough to break into them. So it looks for the honey badger to help. It leads the badger toward the bees' nest. When the honey badger smashes into the nest, the honeyguide can also eat its fill.

83

The hummingbird feeds on flower nectar. Nectar is a sweet liquid made by flowers to attract pollinating insects. It is not always easy for birds to reach, but the hummingbird is able to hover in front of the flower while it sips the nectar using its long tongue.

I DON'T BELIEVE IT!

The hummingbird has to eat lots of nectar to get enough energy to survive. If a human were to work as hard as a hummingbird, he or she would need to eat three times their weight in potatoes each day.

41

Life in snow and ice

85 The coldest places on Earth are the Arctic and the Antarctic. The Arctic is as far north as it is possible to go, and the Antarctic is south, at the bottom of the Earth. The snowy owl is one of the largest birds in the Arctic. Its white feathers hide it in the snow

86 The snow bunting breeds on Arctic islands and farther north than any other bird. The female makes a nest of grasses, moss and lichens on the ground. She lays four to eight eggs and, when they hatch, both parents help to care for the young. Seeds, buds and insects are the snow bunting's main foods.

88 Sheathbills scavenge any food they can find. These large white birds live in the far south on islands close to the Antarctic. They do catch fish but they also search the beaches for any dead animals they can eat. They also snatch weak or dying young from seals and penguins.

Snowy sheathbill

Snow bunting

Snowy owl

Ptarmigan

87 The ptarmigan has white feathers in the winter to help it hide from enemies among the winter snows in the Arctic. But in summer its white plumage would make it very obvious, so the ptarmigan moults and grows brown and grey feathers.

89 **Penguins have a thick layer of fat just under their skin to help protect them from the cold.** Their feathers are waterproof and very tightly packed for warmth. Penguins live mainly in Antarctica, but some live in South Africa, South America and Australia.

Emperor penguin

Tundra swan

QUIZ

All of these birds live in snow and ice, but some of them live in the north and some live in the south. Can you tell which live in the north, the Arctic, and which live in the south, the Antarctic?

All belong in the north, the Arctic, except for the penguins and the snowy sheathbill which belong in the south, the Antarctic.

90 **The tundra swan lays its eggs and rears its young in the tundra of the Arctic.** The female bird makes a nest on the ground and lays up to five eggs. Both male and female care for the young. In autumn the whole family migrates, travels south to spend the winter in warmer lands.

Special beaks

91 **The snail kite feeds only on water snails and its long upper beak is specially shaped for this strange diet.** When the kite catches a snail, it holds it in one foot while standing on a branch or other perch. It strikes the snail's body with its sharp beak and shakes it from the shell.

◀ The snail kite lives in the southern USA, and Central and South America, but it is now very rare.

Toco toucan

93 **The wrybill is the only bird with a beak that curves to the right.** The wrybill is a type of plover which lives in New Zealand. It sweeps its beak over the ground in circles to pick up insects.

92 **The toco toucan's colourful beak is about 19 centimetres long.** It allows the toucan to pick fruit and berries at the end of branches that it would not otherwise be able to reach. There are more than 40 different kinds of toucan, and all have large beaks of different colours. The colours and patterns may help the birds attract mates.

Black skimmer

94 **The lower half of the skimmer's beak is longer than the upper half.** This allows it to catch fish in a special way. The skimmer flies just above the water with the lower part of its beak below the surface. When it comes across a fish, the skimmer snaps the upper part of its beak down to trap the prey.

I DON'T BELIEVE IT!

The flamingo's legs may look as if they are back to front. In fact, what appear to be the bird's knees are really its ankles!

96 **The crossbill has a very unusual beak which crosses at the tip.** The shape of this beak allows the bird to open out the scales of pine cones and remove the seeds it feeds on.

95 **The flamingo uses its beak to filter food from shallow water.** It stands in the water with its head down and its beak beneath the surface. Water flows into the beak and is pushed out again by the flamingo's large tongue. Any tiny creatures such as insects and shellfish are trapped on bristles in the beak.

Birds and people

97 People buying and selling caged birds has led to some species becoming extremely rare. Some pet birds such as budgerigars are bred in captivity, but others such as parrots are taken from the wild, even though this is now illegal. The beautiful hyacinth macaw, which used to be common in South American jungles, is now rare because of people stealing them from the wild to sell.

Red-fan parrot

King parrot

▲ Hyacinth macaw

98 In some parts of the world, people still keep falcons for hunting. The birds are kept in captivity and trained to kill rabbits and other animals, and bring them back to their master. When the birds are taken out hunting, they wear special hoods over their heads. These are removed when the bird is released to chase its prey.

99 Many kinds of birds are reared for their eggs and meat. Chickens and their eggs are a major food in many countries, and ducks, geese and turkeys are also eaten. These are all specially domesticated species but some wild birds, such as pheasants, partridge and grouse, are also used as food.

Starling

100 Starlings are very common city birds. Huge flocks are often seen gathering to roost, or sleep on buildings. Starlings originally lived in Europe and Asia but have been taken to other countries and been just as successful. For example, 100 years ago 120 starlings were released in New York. Now starlings are among the most common birds in North America. The starling is very adaptable. It will eat a wide range of foods including, insects, seeds and fruits, and will nest almost anywhere.

I DON'T BELIEVE IT!

In one city crows wait by traffic lights. When the lights are red they place walnuts in front of the cars. When the lights turn green the cars move over the nuts, breaking the shells. The birds then fly down and pick up the kernels!

Index

A B
American golden plover 23
antbird **41**
Arctic tern **22**, 23
beak **8**, **9**, 15, **18**, 19, 21, 25, **26**, 30, **31**, 38, 39, **40**, **44–45**
bird of paradise **17**, 34
  blue 17
bird of prey **10**, **11** 39
  Andean condor **10**
  collared falconet **11**
  osprey **39**
bowerbird **16**
breeding 11, 14, 16, 32, 36, 37

C D
Canada goose **22**, 23
cassowary 37
cave swiftlet 21
chick 22, **24**, 26, 28, 29, 30, **32–33** 35, 37, 42, 43
cock-of-the-rock 17
Congo peafowl 34, 35
courser **24**
courtship **16–17**
crossbill **45**
cuckoo 21
desert 6, **24–25**
dipper **39**
duck 12, **33**, 46

E F
eagle 8, 31
  bald **20**
  golden **30–31**
  harpy 34
  sea **30**, 31
  snake 30
egg **9**, 13, 16, 20, 21, 22, 24, **27**, **28–29**, 30–31, 32, 36, 38, 42, 46
emu **36–37**
enemy 24, **25–26**, 33, 42
falcon 32, 46
feathers 6, **8**, 9, **16–17**, 18, 19, 21, 24, 25, 26, 32, 34, 35, 42
feet 14, 18, 30, 32, 34, **36**, 37, **39**, 40, **44**
female 10, 16, 17, 20, 21, 32, 34, 36, 37, 38, 42, 43

flamingo **45**
flower 10, 16, **41**
food 9, 10, 13, 19, 20, 22, 23, 24, 25, 28, 29, 31, 32, 33, 34, 35, 37, 38, 39, 41

G H
gannet 15
goose 12, 33, 46
goshawk **9**
great bustard **10**, 11
ground bird **36–7**
guillemot **27**
hawk 8, 32,
heron **38**
hoatzin 35
hornbill **20**
hummingbird 6, **12**, **41**
  bee 6, **10**, 11, 12, 28, 29
honeyguide bird **41**
hunting bird **9**, **12**, **30–31**, 46

J K L
jacana **38**, 39
junglefowl 34
killdeer **26**
kingfisher **38**, 39
kite, snail **44**
kiwi **19**, 28
  brown 29

M N
macaw, hyacinth **46**
mallee fowl 21
mating 8, 13, **16–17**, 20, 44
migration **22–3**
nest 13, 16, **20–21**, 26, 27, 30, 35, 37, 38, 41, 42, 43, 47
nightjar **18**, 19

O
oilbird 19
osprey **39**
ostrich 6, **10**, 11, 28, 29, **36**
owl **18**, 42
  barn **18**, 19
  elf **24**
  snowy **42**

P
parrot 9
  hawk-headed 46
  kakapo **18**, 19
  king **46**
  scarlet macaw 35
partridge 29, 46
  grey 29
peacock **16–17**
pelican **39**
penguin 14, 15, 33, 42, **43**
peregrine falcon **12**, 13
pigeon **32**
poorwill **18**, 19
prey 9, 10, 12, 13, 15, 18, 19, 26, 30, 31, 38, 39, 45, 46
ptarmigan 42

Q R
quetzal 35
rainforest 6, 17, 34, 35, 37
raven **31**
rhea **37**
roadrunner **13**

S T
sandgrouse **24**
skimmer **45**
snow bunting 42
starling **47**
swan **8**, 9, **33** 43
tawny frogmouth 26
thrush, song **9**
toucan, toco **44**
turkey **29**, 46

W V
vulture **10**
  lappet-faced **25**
  lammergeier **25**
wandering albatross **11**, 29
weaver bird **21**
wing 6, **8**, **11**, 12, **13**, 14, 15, 24, **25**, **30–31**
woodpecker **40**
  great spotted 29
wren, cactus 25